I0621626

PRAISE FOR *SEED TO SEEDLING: GROWING IN THE DARKNESS*

In *Seed to Seedling: Growing in The Darkness*, Heather courageously invites us into her sacred grief journey after losing her beloved husband to suicide. While witnessing the birthing of her personal transformational process, we feel encouraged and inspired to keep moving forward to discover our own path of emergence back to the light of our soul. If you are in the throes of grief or loss, this book with its wisdom infused passages, will help to know that you are not alone and that growth is possible, even when we feel eclipsed by the darkness of grief.

Cara Hope Clark, Award-winning author of
Widow's Moon and the
Transformational Nature of Grief

In a stream-of-consciousness style, Heather McBogg's poems invite the reader to walk alongside her in the rawness and transparency of her grief. Her prose offers clarity through the natural world and shows how hope can emerge, though not in the stages we would expect.

Amy Burns, author of
Breast Cancer at 35: A Memoir.

This is a beautifully written book about the painful journey of grief –mourning the death of a beloved spouse. It describes a course that many of us have traveled, enhanced by rich poetry journaling this enormous path through loss. It is also a narrative of a courageous movement towards acceptance of what cannot be changed. In reading this book, I was reminded that the journey of grief is different for each person – painful and unique, and at the end of this difficult journey what you hope for is acceptance and a return of some joyfulness in your life. If you have the courage to read it, you will learn a lot about what it takes to move through grief and have faith that someday things will look brighter. As with her seedling, she is just beginning to grow, another step on this difficult journey.

Tiza Pyle, author of,
Possibilities: Re-framing Life in Your Later Years with the B.A.S.E. Model for Change

Heather's perspective on grief and the seed gave me many "aha" moments as well as feeling like I wasn't alone in some of my crazy thoughts while grieving. Her poetry gave a very defined visual of what she was going through as she grew through her grief process. The seed she speaks of became more corporeal with each chapter I read. I felt like I was watching the full cycle of life as her writing is very visual. I felt like I knew that seed.

Beth Nutter,
Memoir-in-Progress

"Seed to Seedling: Growing in The Darkness is a raw, deeply moving testament to the resilience of the human spirit. Heather McBogg, with her courageous and unflinchingly honest account, becomes a beacon of inspiration for readers. Depicted through deeply

moving poetry and powerful storytelling, her journey through the sudden and stark grief of losing her beloved husband, Duncan, illuminates the dark, often isolating path of sorrow with intense vulnerability.

In the midst of personal tragedy, the world can feel heavy, overwhelming, and devoid of answers. When life unravels unexpectedly, leaving wounds that seem impossible to heal, hope can feel distant—almost unreachable. McBogg's poetic reflections offer a clear and honest exploration of grief, pain, and the crushing weight of loss. Her writing provides no easy answers or quick fixes but rather an unfettered look at the depth of sorrow and the struggle to move forward. For those who find themselves in the darkest of times, here is a space to acknowledge the hardship without the pressure to find the light... just yet.

McBogg's writing is more than just an account of loss; it is a heartfelt exploration of the complex emotions that accompany such a devastating experience. Her words offer profound comfort to those navigating their own losses, providing solace by embracing the pain, confusion, and heartache experienced in the wake of tragedy. Through her story, McBogg shows that even in the darkest moments, the possibility of transformational growth leading to new paths forward remains ever-present.

This book is more than a lyrical memoir—it is a trustworthy companion for anyone who feels lost in grief and a lifeline for those struggling to find meaning or light after tragedy. *Seed to Seedling* reminds us all that while the journey through loss may be painful and dark, the possibility remains for new beginnings, sometimes found in the most unexpected places."

Scott and Josie Gwin, authors of
A Field Guide to Survivor-Centered Care and
Co-founders of The Resilience Resource

SEED

to

SEEDLING

Growing in The Darkness

Heather McBogg

ISBN:
Paperback: 9798991448000
eBook: 9798991448017

Editor and Publishing Consultant: WWW.CSUSANNUNN.COM
Book Interior and E-book Design by Amit Dey (amitdey2528@gmail.com)
Cover Design: Heather McBogg

If you are struggling, please call the Suicide and Crisis Lifeline by dialing 988, caring and compassionate individuals will listen and help you find your way to another day.

DEDICATION

For my beloved Duncan, whose love and generous heart were my home. Your example of self-compassion and span of control will forever live in my heart and mind.

For the warriors, both brave and afraid, choosing to live yet another day and finding connection in this big and topsy-turvy world, you are a light.

For those who walk alongside grieving hearts, you are incredibly invaluable. Your role is among the most vital to the griever. Though at times you may doubt yourself, your very presence and desire to continually show up means more than you could ever imagine.

For those who struggle to find meaning and purpose after the loss of your loved one, keep going, you are not alone on this journey.

TABLE OF CONTENTS

PROLOGUE

He felt like home. The second I met Duncan, my nervous system relaxed as if letting out a sigh of relief. Here was someone who was not afraid of my story and who didn't seem phased by my childhood traumas. Here was a tender man, who calmly listened as I poured out the events of my life up to that point. He did not run from me, tell me I was too much, or seem even remotely phased as my stories unfolded. He took me in, trusted me in return, and shared his own stories with me. Besides my dearest granny, this was the first person in my entire life who I believed wanted to "see" me. His tenderness with me extended into all areas of our growing relationship. We were both seeking connection from someone open to experience life with another wounded wanderer, and we had found one another.

In the early years of our marriage, Duncan's father died by suicide. Duncan handled it the only way he knew how, by turning inward and processing this loss alone. The way this showed up shook our marriage. He would binge drink on weekends with his friends in an effort to numb the shock. I was not sure our marriage would make it through this, but in the end, Duncan chose our marriage, he chose us and quit drinking.

As the years passed and his sobriety stood the test of time, something new was awakening within me. I wanted to start a family. We had not been using contraception for years. I wondered why I was not getting pregnant, but I was so busy starting my career as an art teacher, I didn't have time to give it much thought. Until, at thirty-four, I began to obsess over the idea of having kids. After much testing, I was labeled as having "unexplained infertility." I did have one spontaneous pregnancy after this "diagnosis," which ended in miscarriage. This pregnancy convinced us both, more than ever before, that we truly wanted a family. We went to fertility specialists, who ran so much bloodwork I am surprised I didn't shrivel up into a prune! After several attempts with various medications, we began invitro-fertilization (IVF). My first attempt ended in a miscarriage, and I nearly gave up. This was truly a trying time in our marriage, as we both had become convinced my body was destroying our potential babies. We were so angry at my body, and we both turned on it for a spell. Until one of the most compassionate nurses in the world said, "Heather, your body is amazing. It knew this baby was not viable, it had a trisomy-something-or-other and would never have been able to survive. Your body is doing its job." I wept. Duncan and I clung to each other as we decided to try one more time.

After weeks of countless hormone shots, two embryos were transferred. One little embryo split and I was pregnant with triplets. At the nine-week check, it was discovered the identical twins did not make it, but the third little embryo was growing! During this period, Duncan treated me like a queen. This was a difficult pregnancy, and I was placed on bedrest for the majority of the nine months. About a week after the due date, our beloved first-born son arrived. Other than our wedding day, I had never seen Duncan happier. He worked hard to be the best dad, ever present and his biggest fan. Just over a year later, much to our great surprise, I was pregnant with our second child. Our family was growing.

Duncan and I were learning to trust each other in new ways. Having children seemed to awaken our unhealed parts. We had to look our fears in the face as the mirror our children became revealed to us the parts we had exiled, the parts we had never healed. Our survival drives kicked into full gear and we both became hypervigilant in our own unique ways. Many of these patterns which served us in our youth now led to anxious fears and ruminating minds. We simply did not see what was happening and suffered in our own worlds as we tried to be the perfect parents.

Perfectionism was a lifelong theme. Duncan saw it and called it out when he noticed its new iterations. He once grew very uneasy as I taught our boys a song from my childhood, the lyrics went like so: "Practice makes perfect, practice makes perfect. The longer I practice the better I'll be." The old song included a kiddo learning to play the piano and messing up repeatedly. He obstinately butted into the conversation and said, "Practice makes better." Perfectionism was a dominating theme throughout Duncan's life. As a child gymnast, he had been awarded a "perfect ten" for a routine he had completed at age twelve. By the time he was in college, he acknowledged the harmful impact this had on him. He had grown to believe he could achieve perfection. It took him years to learn self-compassion and span of control, and once he experienced letting go, he began to speak these concepts to others. He did not want others to suffer as he had in his quest for perfection.

In February of 2021, during the height of COVID, Duncan found his dream job at Stanford University. After nine grueling virtual interviews, he was offered the position as *Director of Online Education*. During the process of packing, purging belongings, looking for a place to stay, teaching our children virtually, and preparing to leave the state of our birth to move across the country, some switch inside of Duncan was flipped.

My previously strong, confident, and supportive husband stopped sleeping and began to change. Within weeks of accepting the position, he was almost unrecognizable. By the end of April, it was clear we were not going anywhere. We had sold our home, and he had quit his job; this broke him further and he began to sink into a dark hole of distortions. We sought help, but due to COVID, the help he received was woeful at best. Seeking repair through a cocktail of prescribed medications that fried his nervous system and a virtual *Intensive Outpatient Program* that asked him daily if he was suicidal, he languished. None of these systemic supports offered him what he really needed, a place for his nervous system to be seen and held.

The constant focus on suicidality sent him further into a spiral of cognitive distortions and he was unable to see how we could find our way through this. He was angry at himself and could not hear any encouragement to the contrary. In his mind, he failed our family. He told me one day, "Honey, I know I am sick because I don't see you or the boys anymore." This terrified me, but I naively believed we could work our way through this as we had so many other hurdles throughout our 21-year marriage.

The medications they put him on gave him a movement disorder we assume was Tardive Dyskinesia. He was in physical agony on top of his mental anguish. Instead of removing the medication, the doctors prescribed more medications which were meant to mask his symptoms. It was absolute torture to watch, and I wanted him off the medications so badly. But he was a grown man, and I wanted to support any autonomy he could muster. In the end, the weekly changes in his medications and the unbearable side effects they produced were what stole any hope that remained.

In June of 2021, my beloved Duncan took his own life.

After the initial shock wore off, flashbacks of moments during his illness began to flood me. In one memory, I remember peeking down the stairwell to check on him during one of his meetings. I saw his fingers furiously typing away on the keyboard of his computer, he was writing something. I wondered if he had written me a farewell note or some last words for our boys. I went to his computer and started digging around. I found a google doc he had edited just a few days before he died. I pulled it up. He wrote many things about his father, his interviews and receiving the Stanford job, he wrote painful accounts about his hospital stays, but there was one section in particular I felt he wrote for us all. It was titled, *The Pitfalls of Perfection:*

"I've since come to realize that Stanford was just an extension of the value I've inadvertently held onto since I was 12. The idea that perfection is possible and achievable. When I was 12, I got a "perfect 10" on the horizontal bar at a regional gymnastics competition. The idea that nobody is perfect left my universe and I began a long journey of internalizing perfectionism as not only an achievable goal, but a potential reality with which to live. Obviously, people are correct when they say nobody is perfect and perfection isn't possible, but no one could tell that to the 12-year-old who did it. Unfortunately, over the years, no one could get that to sink into the adult that I had become either. In hindsight, Stanford was just another extension of the search for perfection as opposed to a recognition that I had it pretty damn good already, and that good enough was a perfectly viable and in fact preferred option. In this particular case, my perfectionism created an almost impenetrable wall of self-loathing and regret that seems almost unsurmountable."

The demons my beloved battled, were ones so many of us face as we strive to be the best versions of ourselves and live meaningful lives. We hope to pass on a legacy to our children we can be proud of. In the end, my love had lost the values he held most, self-compassion and relaxing into the span of control allotted to us. His illness and the medications stole him away.

I speak often and frequently to whomever will listen, about the truths of suicide. Many view it as a weakness, a selfish act, or as a loss of faith or belief. I adamantly argue none of this is true. I believe the majority of people who end up taking their own lives are unwell. I firmly believe they left their body long before and illness drove their choices. Here is the thing, illness, overmedication, not feeling heard or seen by the professionals you've entrusted yourself to, living in distorted thinking – it steals you away from your body. It creates a dark veil behind which all you know and love is lost. It steals all hope and kills you from the inside out.

My husband did not selfishly end his life. I know this because when he was well, he said he could never do to our boys what his father did to him. He lived and breathed for them, wanting to be the best dad he could be. He was not a perfect human, but he was a loyal and loving one, and that is how I choose to remember him. His illness and death remain a tragedy.

This book portrays the continuing progression of my changing relationship with Duncan and myself as I grieve. Grief is changing me. Losing Duncan in such a manner has left me as a seed produced by our former life, sending me falling through the liminal space between past comforts and present grief, plunging me deep into the cold, hard ground, surrounded by darkness. The very nature of who I am has impacted the germination of this seed. In the darkness, the truths of impermanence began to dance about in my mind; impressing upon my heart how the present moment is all we truly have, and it is incredibly precious. Come, join me on the journey of my early years of grief as reflected through the lens of the germination of the seed produced by my marriage to Duncan.

INTRODUCTION

Nature itself can be one of the most healing entities in grief. It requires us to be in the present moment so we may discern the gifts life has to offer us. It is easy to get lost in the beauty created by the sunlight as it casts its rays through the leaves of the trees or how it dances upon the water, animating this life-giving element. The soughing of the wind and songs of the birds, the rustle of creatures in the grasses and croaking of frogs in a marsh, the whoosh of wings as birds fly over the water or the screeching of the hawks high above as they circle; these are only perceived when one pays attention and is awakened to the present moment in front of them.

In my grief, I have found solace within nature. Being present with it has created moments of awe as I gaze upon the miracles that surround me. My soul finds rest in the stories of connectivity and interdependence witnessed through the relationships found within nature. I find correlations to my past and present moments, while anxiously awaiting future ones. I am filled with breathtaking wonder as I witness the sun glisten on the tip of dewy grass or the frost on snow covered trees. I feel myself exhale as the heron glides upon the water's surface, wings arcing in beautiful repose. Herons are a gentle sign following me since my youth – reminding me I am not alone. Hopeful wonder fills me as the hawk screeches and circles above our home with its family, as if Duncan himself were watching us through their eyes. The theatrical dance of nature as it tickles the senses: feeling the smoothness of a rock in my hand and the cool breeze causing my hair to tickle my cheek, the salty taste of ocean air when gifted time away, and the smell of blossoms adorning Colorado's trees in the spring, visions of blue and orange sunsets filling the sky, and the sounds of songbirds, winds and lakeshore waves. The interplay between plants, animals and the elements create incredible beauty and an unfolding story of how one depends upon the other. How can one, even in their grief, not stop and exist in the present moment when surrounded by such beauty? It is the calling of our wild hearts to "live" in the midst of our pain. It is our love for the ones we lost beckoning us to engage with all that is before us. Nature demands it, but the rest of life requires us to choose it – to choose to apply the lessons of nature to our everyday life.

It is true, there are moments in grief, where seeing and being present feels impossible. Our systems may turn inward because the pain is too great, blinding us to the outer world. Many experience fear of connecting because we may once again lose that which we love. Waking up each day and choosing life is an act of bravery when our hearts are broken. We begin to meet, as we step into each new day, our inner warrior, who is determined to fight for us. Our warrior is strong and brave, not because it must be, rather it is this way because it feels the pull toward the energy that courses through all things and needs connection. It is in seeing this where we no longer see the need for strength as a painful reminder of what was lost; rather, we can begin to see it as a way to connect to our lost loved one. We can begin to feel the transformational power of allowing our love for them to nurture our very soul. We can see while in the depth of the dark soil, we are still able to be sustained by their great love. This in turn begins the interdependence, the dance which exists for all living things. It is in our weakest moments where our inner strength is discovered.

The germination process of a seed presents so many beautiful opportunities to reflect upon how we, ourselves, are growing beings, planted into various soils and in various climates. Each of us, a very different seed, produced by a multitude of conditions and in need of various supports for our growth. And though this will look different for each of us, there are a few elements all seeds need: nutrient rich soil, water, oxygen, and sunlight. What each has to offer is akin to the connection we receive from friends, family, and helpers who come alongside us on our journey. Each granting us the gift of what we need to expand and grow in different stages of our individual healing journey. None of the healing is linear and always ebbs and flows as we find what resources help us grow and as we learn to adapt to our seasons of rest and restore.

The writing in this book demonstrates the wisdom I have gathered up to this point. I will continue to learn as this is an ongoing and lifelong journey. The poems are a mixture of nature revealing her truths and instances of inner struggle as I wrestle with the monumental task of grieving my best friend, while trying to stay present for our boys. They reflect times when my beloved used nature to visit me and heal my heart, breathing life back into me. They capture periods in the dark soil, as I processed the loss of who I once was and the dreams I once held, so I might walk into what is. They show moments of curiosity and strength in tandem with those of fear, regret, and anger. For these are the way of grief, the constant ebb and flow of the tides of life bringing us to and away from what is – growing us into the light of the sun.

Each section begins with the story of a seed, which fell from a mother plant, who had not yet reached its potential. This seed's journey of becoming a seedling is a representation of my process of being carried away from the plant of my marriage and finding myself inside the soil of the unknown. It is here in the soil where the lessons I share began. This is my journey toward healing and the beginning of a new story.

The Dance

I hear your songs
Your cries
They call to me
Calling me to ground
To earth
To sky
To sea
Making my heart soar
To join yours
To journey
Beyond self
Ego
No longer silent
I hear you
I can never unhear you
No longer seeking the why
Seeing only momentum
Not looking back
Only forward
Inner warrior
Subdued
With time
Broken histories
Past beauty rising
Anew
You sit beside me
Whispering your truths
My heart hears
My soul cries

With yours
Joining you
Not fighting for you
Rather alongside
Listening
Learning
Soaking in your great wisdom
Your truth
Universal truths
Of wholeness
Of unity
Balance
Embracing the dark
As part of the light
The winds blow in
We soar high
Above it all
Viewing with fresh eyes
Beauty in the pain
Seeing the sleepwalkers
With grace
As their silence
Was once mine
Helplessness shed
Spirit awoke
Hopeful warmth
The sun
Shining down
Dancing with the moon
Through days
And nights

Weather patterns
Come and flow
Shaping us
Making us
The connectivity
Undeniable
All life
Part of the source
Of God
Of Universe
Of the Great Spirit
Many names
Giver of energy
Of light
Of substance
Love is your cry
Your power
Healing
Creating
Reaching out
Beyond comprehension
Grief bore in me a seed
This seed is taking root
Becoming
Enlightening
Empowering

January 11, 2022

SECTION ONE

PLANTED IN THE DARK: DORMANCY

Story of a Seed, Part One

You died and at that moment, our life together died too. You unraveled and slowly withered before fully growing to maturity. However, you produced a seed, a single solitary seed. As you exhaled your last breath, the seed was released from the grip of the beloved mother plant.

Falling through liminal spaces between the past and whatever was to come, the seed was set forth on a mission – find rich soil, supportive soil, or perish. It was an intrinsic knowing, the seed had to find a safe place to grow.

The winds came and the seed felt itself carried away and pulled along the gentle currents of this beautiful and well-intentioned friend. Their journey together weaved them in and out of cold and icy places and back into warm and comfortable ones, until the seed departed and landed on the ground.

A beautiful grackle saw the seed and swallowed it whole. Cast into a warm and oddly comforting place, co-mingling with other seeds and berries, the seed became curious. "What shall become of me?" Unsure of its safety, the seed felt relieved when it was evacuated. Through the air it fell, encased in a warm, milky hug, and landed on the cold, firm soil below with a jolt felt throughout its entire core. Stunned, the seed could only lay there, staring up at the blue sky watching the birds fly and feeling the warmth of the sun once again.

No longer inside the belly of the grackle, the seed took a moment and shook off its shock, finding safety on the ground. Its old friend, the wind, came and blew soil, dust, leaves, and other debris over it, blanketing it. The seed rested under the protection of the steady layering.

The darkness came as more and more debris blanketed the seed. A new sensation began to fill the seed's inner core, loneliness came and a stirring of memories of the mother plant swelled within. The stories of its origin lived deep in the cells that made up the soft insides of the seed. The stories created a growing pressure within, and the seed was afraid of what those memories might become. The muffled sounds of the world above reminded the seed of the safety it had felt growing on the limb and the freedom while being carried in the wind; it ached to feel the wind and the sunlight again.

It sat alone within itself as memories, desires, fears, and anxiety of all the potential it possessed ached to be released.

The Process

In this dormant season, buried in the dark soil, we must wait patiently. The shock of early grief is processed so differently for each of us. Like the seed, the length of dormancy is highly dependent upon the type of seed we are. For germination to occur, some seeds need the cold, while others require heat, other seeds need light, while others gather their resources within the darkness. All seeds need moisture, but when it comes and how much there is, is an important factor for germination. For the griever, there are those who must have the light and warmth of supportive relationships at all stages, while others need to come in and out of it, gathering their own resources from the "soil" they are planted within.

Experiences from our past formed a coat upon the seed of us. These determined if our coats are thick and difficult to penetrate, from years of having to be strong, or if they are thin and easily broken, because of hardships that made us feel broken, or barely existent from being handed everything with such ease, or if our coat exists somewhere in-between because of supportive growing. Growth and healing can only begin if that coat is broken open. The time in the dark, in the dormant season determines how our coat will expand and absorb life-giving nutrients which will allow us to grow. It is vital to our existence that we find supportive environments in which to be planted. We must learn to recognize and listen to what the core of our seed is asking, choosing wisely where we plant ourselves. And if we find we have been planted in hostile environments, we must gain the courage to move the seed of our lives into better soil.

In grief, it is easy to get lost in our thoughts or the strong feelings that creep upon us. Often, we who grieve, fail to see the beauty that surrounds unless we intentionally look for it. At times, beauty sneaks in anyway, and shakes us awake – as we often are in a trance of remembering. We want to remember them, yet often the memories are of the last days when the lost one was suffering or struggling through some mental or physical battle. This remembering stirs in us our own battle, often reawakening feelings of powerlessness and fear that were experienced as we watched our loved one suffer. It is easy to get overwhelmed with waves of regret, shame, bitterness, and sorrow. Our minds want to make sense of something that feels utterly inconceivable; they were here, and now they are not. This can drive us toward numbness, hopelessness, difficulties reintegrating, and extreme loneliness. This is the seed experiencing the darkness of the soil surrounding it.

Stigmatized loss can usher in a whole host of battles for our mind and our ability to continue to live meaningful lives. When the means of the loss is either viewed by those around us, or even by ourselves, as something sinful or wrong, the tendency is to self-isolate or take the defense. It is a natural reaction, and it is our mind's way of protecting us from unwanted judgment. However, we thrive in supportive communities. We thrive when we are seen. We thrive when we get out into the world and interact, allowing our story and our humanness to be witnessed. And yet, for this growth and thriving to occur, we often must go through periods of dormancy.

While healing, it is helpful to also witness ourselves, sitting with our stories, feelings, and reactions. Sometimes this is best done in moments of solitude, other times it is essential to do it in the support of friends, family, or therapists who can remind us of what is true. In our solitude, we sit with our *internal family* – the many *parts* of our self that appear as we process our grief. At times, we may meet some uncomfortable characters in our storytelling. Often, we discover some variations of an internal judge who is ready to convict us at every turn, a child who is cowering in fear, anxious *parts* that worry about what will come, a dreamer who gets caught up in grandiose thinking, or insecurity causing us to shrink and become small. These are only a few examples, and it is important to note that all these *parts* are here to protect us.

As we grieve, these *parts* come to the forefront and try to keep us safe in whatever capacity we learned to allow them to operate. Sometimes these *parts* conflict, and it becomes very difficult to stay present and sort out what is truth versus what are old stories that no longer fit. As we sit with these, we are often composing new stories to make sense of what happened. This work can be difficult to do in solitude and often requires us to reach out for help. Grief not only exists within our present loss but can stir up old unresolved wounds from our past and reveals how our *internal family* has been keeping us safe. What once worked to keep us safe and in homeostasis, may no longer work, and our grief can potentially become complicated.

However, it is in the dark places where we can also find our strength. It is there where we may come to peace with our *parts* and evaluate the stories we have accepted with curiosity. It is there in the darkness where we face our humanness and grow in the understanding that death and loss, pain and trauma are as much a part of life as the process of birth – of being a seed planted into the soil. It is not in the letting go of, but the absorbing and acceptance of these aspects of life, where we may begin to find freedom from the crippling pain of grief. Grief presents duality, and dichotomies can and do exist. While in the midst of devastation, life chases us. Grief is a beautifully enlightened sage if we dare to look her bravely in the face and experience the feelings she stirs up.

The swirling of emotions and memories she brings pulls us from the present moment. She may take us into a past where unfathomably precious moments and opportunities may have been missed. Reflective states usher in a struggle between learning lessons from what was, and what currently is – the precious moments that sit in front of us right now at present. It is difficult to rock back and forth in this space, so we might become free. In creating a visual of being stuck in the mud, my therapist spoke to my grief. Through her gentleness she reminded me we cannot press the gas hard and fast to be released, we will only dig in deeper. Instead, we must rock back and forth to regain momentum. That rocking of pressing into the pain and experiencing it in tolerable amounts, then safely rocking back out and reacclimating to the present moment, back and forth until movement can occur. This is not a process you can rush. This is what grief does to us. Though scary, she becomes a beloved granny soothing our worries by rocking us within loving and safe arms. Guiding us toward feeling and healing. It just takes time.

The poems in this section reveal my struggle in the darkness. The wrestling with my memories, beliefs, and the exquisite pain of losing my love to suicide.

If Only

If only you hadn't seen that posting
If only you had been content with what you had
If only you hadn't said yes
If only our previous discussion had borne more weight
If only my initial reaction had been heeded
If only I hadn't been dazzled by your newfound faith
If only I had truly listened to you
Beyond your words
If only I had seen you beyond my own experiences
If only I had set aside my stubborn desires
If only I had been more flexible with your changing tides
If only I had understood your cries
If only I had taken heed
If only the circumstances hadn't been so convincing
If only the external signs hadn't played a role
If only I had paid more attention to your signs
If only the sleepless nights had been interpreted accurately
If only the spiritual side had never entered
If only reason had ruled
If only I had stopped for a moment long enough
If only I had seen things differently
If only I hadn't felt overwhelmed
If only I hadn't been ruled by my to do list
If only I had held on to my initial reaction
If only I hadn't pushed so hard for "your dream"
If only I saw your dream was what we already had
If only COVID hadn't set the stage
If only other people's stories were just that
If only I hadn't jumped on board

If only I had followed my instincts
If only I had asked more questions
If only I had put a lid on my own emotions
If only I had insisted the meds stop
If only my attempts had worked
If only your mind hadn't gone so dark
If only you had found self-compassion
If only you had seen hope
If only I had been better at encouraging
If only you had accepted you did nothing wrong
If only your distortions weren't so loud
If only you listened to your body
If only your mind had allowed that
If only our system hadn't failed us all
If only you had known your value and worth
If only my fear hadn't taken over
If only the chaos hadn't overwhelmed
If only I had known what to do
If only the helplessness hadn't been so strong
If only I had stopped and loved on you more
If only you hadn't pushed us away
If only your wisdom of self-compassion transferred
If only your body hadn't been made ill from the meds
If only I had acted faster
If only you weren't in so much pain
If only you saw a different way out
If only I had held you more
If only I had known what to do for you
If only you hadn't made up your mind
If only I had stayed home
If only you hadn't demanded some time alone

If only those 15 minutes hadn't been granted
If only the bar had broken
If only she could have gotten you down
If only I had answered that call
If only I had been faster
If only you saw life as a better alternative
If only

July 22, 2021

The progression of his illness was so incredibly fast and often I found myself feeling like my head was humming in a confused state. I did not understand that my nervous system was trying to protect me from the intensity of the situation as it was unraveling. When he was gone, and the plant that had been our marriage and our family was ripped out of the soil, a lonely seed fell into the space between what was and what was to come. The seed began a journey and when it landed, went deep enough to begin the germination process. It was filled with memories, stored deep inside the embryo and covered with a thick coat of protection. As the cold darkness of early grief threatened to steal away all life, the waters of friendship came in, surrounding me with the presence of mind to hold on to hope. Amidst the hope, deep inside however, swirled all the fears, worries, and finger pointing voices of shame and blame.

You

You are gone and I can't,
I just can't.
I can't understand or make sense of this.
I'm supposed to carry this thing,
this massive emptiness.
I don't know how.
I'm so very lost in the emptiness I carry.
You left and a vacuum of space came and sucked you away,
all of you.
I look for you,
and find nothing.

You stole yourself away from me.
I can't find you anymore.
Pictures and memories feel distant,
other,
as though they belong to another.
I cannot connect to them,
and it hurts so much.

The darkness didn't just steal you,
it stole comfort,
security,
home,
my best friend,
a father,
a son,
a mentor,
a beloved.

It stole mindfulness.
It stole all of you.

Where the hell are you?

I find only darkness,
confusion,
illness.

It consumes me from the inside, out.

I'm hollowed out and left bare,
naked,
vulnerable,
raw.

I cannot think clearly.

No longer seeking comfort from friends,
I lay within myself.
So damn lost without you.
I scarcely trust myself,
you were my compass.
Without you I spiral.

I can't.
Really, I just can't.
How do I navigate in the darkness you left?

My tears drown me.
I'm not sure I'm reaching for safety lines,

or if I'm being sucked under the current of tears.
I'm lost in the current,
tumbled to unrecognition.
Up is down,
and down is dark.
I'm stuck,
caught in this trap.

Where are you?

I need you!

I'm so afraid.

October 6, 2021

Shower

I step into the safety of the warmth.
It covers and touches me,
every part of me.

I lean in,
caressing the wall with my hands.
I begin to weep
as I feel its coldness.

The warmth on my body,
juxtaposed with the cold
hard ceramic tiles on my hands and forehead.

The shower has become my safe space,
to feel,
to weep,
to question.

The tile on the wall,
a poor substitute for your chest.
Yet, I lean in.
Hands flat and holding you,
but it's not you,
and I weep uncontrollably.

Your embrace - the warm water -
pours over me and I stand there,

head on the tile,
asking why?
Why did you leave me?

Was I not enough?
Was I a poor wife?
Lover?
Friend?

Was I blind?
Did I not see?
Did I not love you well enough?

If I could pound my way through this wall to you,
I would.

I am so alone now.
The shower grows cold
and I, so empty.

October 9, 2021

Drowning

I give myself space to be human
when all I see are mistakes,
many missed opportunities,
regrets.

How does a person work their way out of that?
Wrap their head around that?
How does a person find grace for their humanness?

How do I hold space for the reality that I, too,
was reacting to fear? Confusion.
That I was shutting down after carrying so much weight.

This perfect storm of circumstances became more than
I could carry.
And I struggled to find balance.
To think clearly about how to support the person who
carried me many times.

How do I not see this as my greatest failure?

I'm drowning.

I am so lost.
I awake and can barely breathe.
I look where you should be,
and find emptiness beside me.

I reach out and grasp the air.

But even it is not there.

I gasp, searching for breath,
for a reprieve.

But all I find is an ocean of tears.
They fill my lungs as they roll down my cheeks.
I feel myself drowning.

My chest grows heavy,
and my heart quickens with fear.

My mind races with thoughts.
none are intelligible.

I've lost you, even the memories of you, the feeling of you.

Darkness.
Heavy.
Weighty.
All consuming.

Where are you?
Even my mind has lost you.

Weeping.
Weeping.
Weeping.
I'm drowning.

October 11, 2021

Grasping For Memories

I heard your voice today,
when your mom didn't answer.
It stopped my thoughts.
I was driving through the tears.
Your voice brought you back,
along with my fears.

I had been losing you,
your memory so far.
It's not been that long.
It took driving in this car,
down the crowded highway,
and the sound of your voice
brought you straight to my heart.

I distract and I stray,
my mind has been staying away.
The pain is too great.
I get lost easily
when I'm on my own.
I stare at screens and create stories
because my love,
you left us too soon.

When I close my eyes,
the memories flood me.
The night is no friend,
it tortures me so.
The what ifs and why's,

and questions of how--
I shut them out
Because when I allow,
they shatter and shake me.
I can't let them break me.

We've these two precious souls,
half you and half me.
They need me now.
When I feel broken down,
they don't understand.
I can't show them how.

I love and I hate you.
No, I never could hate you.
But the thought enters now,
as I hate what's been lost.
Why did you leave us?
We need your spirit.

You balanced the scales.
Now our weight is too heavy.
Without you here,
we've tipped and we've toppled.

We distract and we stray.
Our minds staying away.
The pain is too great.
We get lost easily.
In quiet times,
we stare at screens watching stories

because my love,
You left us too soon.

You left us too soon.

October 20, 2021

There are times when memories seem so distant, when they seem to have vanished. At other times, the past feels like someone else's life, and a griever simply cannot connect to who they were when their loved one was alive. However, there are also times when painful memories of illness replace all the other memories, as if this was the only life ever lived with this person. The impact of this traumatic response varies widely depending on the day, the hour, or the minute. I often find myself feeling completely disconnected from life before he became ill. In these moments, I look at photos to ground myself back into truth or spend time with our children – the greatest gift from the love we shared. I call upon friends to retell stories, so I know I am not in fact losing him. He was real.

Birthday Stirrings

Today was our baby's birthday.
He's eight, can you believe it?
Eight years ago today, you held me,
with my head buried deep in your chest.
My hands squeezing yours
as the waves of labor overcame me.

You'd have been singing to him, building Legos with him,
holding him.

My love, I miss you.

Why did you steal yourself away from us?

I'm not meant to be alone.
I'm so terribly lonely now.

Angry.

I've been distracted lately,
not letting myself feel.
I can't stand the hole that surrounds me.
You filled so much of my space
and now empty, I fall.
I'm falling so fast.
I'm scared without you.
I can't trust myself.
My mind has hidden you
protecting me from the pain.

But I hate this protection.
It's not real.
It won't last.
It will only make it greater when I do feel again.

Why did you steal yourself away?
You took our hearts with your last breath.
You brought more pain than you could have ever imagined.
Why did you give up?
Why did you lose sight of us?
You did not protect us from what was happening to you,
you made it our last memory of you
and now we are stuck in it.

We can't escape it.
It's all that comes,
taunting us with its lies,
convicting us with its what ifs and should haves.

October 22, 2021

Too Much Space

Again, I awake
with the expectation that you are there, next to me.
Then as my eyes open
and truth engulfs me,
the loneliness rushes in.
Alone.
So alone.

I play games in my mind.
What was I doing last year at this time?
Living obliviously?
Going about searching for calm?
Finding spaces for myself in the early hours.

Now, there is too much space.

I wish you were here
next to me.
so I could roll over and snuggle in –
a luxury lost on many who are long married
as they crave autonomy,
as they desire space,
as they wrestle with petty irritations.

The space I took, I now resent.
The space I gave, ill advised.
I am not good at being alone anymore.

November 11, 2021

Juggling

In the early morning hour,
I wake once again.
Haunted by your last days with us,
I feel my fear again.
I re-experience how terrified and helpless I felt –
powerless to help you,
to convince you,
that your thoughts were filled with lies.
I shut down.
I had too many glass balls to juggle
Juggling was your thing, not mine,
I was never good at it.
I kept trying to keep the ball that was our boys from crashing
down.
But your ball,
it was lost.
I couldn't find it
until it was shattered all around me.
I missed my chance.
You died alone and among strangers.
You deserved so much more.
You would have never left me alone.
Why did you reassure me?
Why did I leave?
Why did you do it in the house with our baby?
The evil that took you is vile.
It came to steal, kill, and destroy –
to devour you.
You!

Why you?
You were the most beautiful man I've ever known –
strong and kind.
You kept me afloat so often.
I'm terrified about who I am without you.
Why?
Why did you leave us?
I miss you every second.
Even in the vast times of numbness,
when I can't feel you,
when I feel so distant from the memories of you.
I know the depth of the numb matches the depth of my pain.
My system is trying to protect me.
They say in time, this will thaw,
pieces of you will return.
So far, It's just the painful pieces.
I miss your presence –
your energy that created fun,
your play with our babies,
your hand on mine,
your kiss,
your arms around me,
the safety of you.
I miss you!
YOU!

November 25, 2021

Dark Moments

Why is life so fucking cruel to me?
Stealing my innocence at birth
and continually raping my heart,
teasing me with the beautiful
and snatching it away.
Sometimes quickly and quietly as a thief.
Other times, in long drawn-out sagas.
Hand in hand we walk,
loss and myself.
I even lost myself.
It's as if loss enclosed me,
Swallowed me whole.
All I do seems so void of me.

December 5, 2021

I have heard many stories from other stigmatized loss survivors; and a common thread for so many of us is the way the wounds and traumas of our past seem to surface as we process this loss. Grief has such an interesting way of touching every single facet of our lives. It seems to come like a fire, refining all the bits of us that are so incredibly tender. Great loss dredges up other losses, stirring up similar reactions from our past, habits of thought once created to keep us safe. So often, we find these to be suffocating and we lose ourselves. Who am I now? Have I ever known the answer to this question? Have I always been the sum of protective parts trying to keep me safe? Now, as I am on my own again, I realize the role these parts played in my identity. The way he filled my space and the vastness of his absence, makes me acutely aware of this psychology at work inside me.

Abandoned

My shepherd left us wanting
and the waters were not still.
They stirred and boiled
as sickness of mind grew,
unable to heal.
We walked through the valley,
in deaths shadows –
and the evil did not flee.
No rod, nor staff could comfort,
a broken promise to uphold thee.
The battle it grew fierce
until finally you did succumb.
And life now leaves us reeling,
Sitting in the numb.

I'm not quite sure where He did go,
but to your aid, was naught.
For this battle
just we few,
we fought and fought and fought.

January 5, 2022

The Darkness

Darkness Comes
It stole you whole away
It was quiet
Disequilibrium
Dizzying
It wants me too
I feel it
Clawing about
Breathing its foul breath down my neck
Reaching in
Tearing me from the inside out
Whispering its lies
Twisting my thinking
Tempting
Testing
Suffocating
Heavy on my chest it sits
Toying with me
Leaning on my throat
Touching every cell
Judging
Shaming
Maiming
Burying me from the inside out
Filling me with weighty doubt
Gagging me once I'm full
Unable to move
It's too heavy
I'm too heavy

The blanket starts to cover me
And my hands are bound
No sound
No movement
Only tears streaming down my cheeks
I let go
It's too much

January 16, 2022

The endlessness of the dark while waiting for the season to bring more warmth and sunlight often feels so unrelenting in grief. Keeping one's wits and hoping for something to shift, to expand, sometimes feels so incredibly far from the realm of possibility. There are moments when we truly feel ourselves slipping away; when falling asleep becomes a swirl of anxious thoughts threatening all forms of destruction and devastation, and the fact of present safety is completely lost. Often a good long cry, filled with silent screams into the dark, offers the release we need to stand back up. Wiping away our snot filled tears onto our sleeves, we somehow manage to rise again. Opening the curtains to let the daylight back in, we stand there naked in the rawness of our emotions. We the brave, rise and walk into another moment without them. "We are not strong," we tell ourselves; we are surviving. I am learning they are one in the same. It is incredibly brave and requires strength to survive. It is a narrative shift many of us find along the way. In early grief however, it feels ludicrous.

In Need of More than a Sliver

Grief
An endless dark night
With only the sliver of the moon
My soul peers up
Wishing the light would be brighter
The disconnect
The separation
The loss of a soulmate
Is like two cold hands thrust into my chest
Pulling out darkness
While finding no end to it
Folding in unto itself
Kneading it
The words of friends
Mere whispers
In the volume of the depth

January 21, 2022

The words of those who come to walk beside us, often fall into a dark chasm of shock and pain. We feel their presence and intention more than we hear their words at times. We can feel their love for us as they help us with tasks, as they break bread with us and take off whatever weight they can from our shoulders. Very few words seem to break the barrier of pain in the early days, and often the words that do cut through, are the words that hurt. While I was spared a great deal of the hurtful things other grievers have had to endure, such as blame, thoughtless comments, and lack of empathy – all of which seem to be common for so many stigmatized loss survivors – the things I did incur left me feeling impassioned to speak up. Learning to offer grace to others when we are in our darkest moment is such a common experience and a very confusing one. However, it is a way of survival, a protector part arriving to help us stay connected.

The Loop

In the early hours I wake
Flashes of those last months
Return
And torment me
The fear
The terror
The sense of betrayal
You were tortured
By distortions
Lies
Lies of the darkest kind
Stripping you of your truth
Your value
Your stubborn strength
Your sleep
The darkness grew stronger
No prayer
No drug
No mindful activity
No meditation
Could calm you
Your body echoed your thoughts
In a monstrous
Caged lion way
You wandered in repetitive fury
Repeating the question
"How could I have done this?"
Beating yourself up
On a loop

I couldn't stop this vicious wheel
I couldn't intervene in your spiral
I couldn't help
I was as powerless as you
To the beast of unnecessary shame
So very angry at yourself
No voice of reason could penetrate
Damn, if only I could've
If only I could have loved you out of it
Awakened you
Why couldn't I help you?
Why was our love not enough?
Why did you stop seeing even our boys?
I miss you
Every
Single
Second

February 5, 2022

When the love of your life, who was always steady and calm, becomes ill, you are asked to change your role with them. Mental illness is such a scary and frightening turn of events and getting your mind to switch from a partner to a caretaker is a daunting task. Unlike other illnesses, where the outside world understands the route cancers and diseases take, mental illness carries a stigma not only for the afflicted, but for those who love them. Often it is seen as a choice, as witnessed in cases of addiction or it is seen as a weakness of character for those with mental illness. This stigma is a result of a society who is afraid. Fear has such a way of building barriers and causing further pain. One would never say to a person dying of cancer, "Why did you choose this?" or to their partner, "Why are you staying by their side?" These words are common to hear in cases of addiction or mental illness, as if these individuals are somehow unworthy of love. The pain of losing someone to an illness they themselves did not wish to have, an illness that literally stripped them of their dignity, was for me one of the most terrifying experiences. I was utterly powerless and watching the darkness overtake him broke my heart every single day. I even struggle to write about it because that was not him. He was the kindest and most generous person I knew. Grappling with this leaves me lost so often.

Sleepless Nights

All through the night
I awake
Panicked
That you are gone
Some nights are just like that

I lay with My heart racing
Wanting to cry
And sometimes
I can

The growing
All consuming
Knowledge

You are gone

I'm alone

No longer feeling safe
No longer knowing my place
Filled with emptiness
It grows inside me

So, I write
I write to let it out

But the pulsing in my chest
Steals my breath
I tremble

Closing my eyes
I try to find my breath
To calm and center

My hand reaches for you
And I find our sweet pup
Who has taken your place next to me
Small comfort
But I'll take it

February 6, 2022

4 A.M.

Every morning
Around 4 a.m.
I wake
From dreams
Often of you
But not always
And my first utterance
Is your name
The first thought
You
Then often
The words
"I miss you!"
Tumble out
Sometimes with tears
Others, a pillow hug
As the sadness inside floods

Grief does not stop
It does not fade
It does not get better with time
It exists
Always
Alongside memories
Sounds
Smells
Our old haunts
Photos
Our children
Your mom

Loneliness
The ever present
Gaping hole
That maimed spot
Where you once existed
Amputated

Missing you
Inadequately portrays what's deep inside
I'm lacking air
The breath of life
Your life

I just completely
And totally feel empty
You were the presence
That sparked energy
That sparked life
You were my safe place
Every second I feel unsafe now

March 8, 2022

Where To Put My Love

Where does one put their love,
when the love of their life dies?
Where is it supposed to go?
The love lives on
and in the early stages of grief,
it energizes
and pulls you through,
to survival.
And in survival,
it holds you,
for a spell,
cradling you through the rough moments.
But then,
something shifts –
it sits there,
Longing,
Lonely,
Scared,
Confused.
This powerful life force
needs to know,
where do I go now?

June 9, 2022

While sitting in the darkness, acknowledging the gaping hole left behind as the result of our loss, many grievers wonder where they are supposed to put their love? Where is it supposed to go when the receiver is no longer with us? This love is not for anyone else. It is unique to that individual. So, the love sits on us, heavily; like the darkness of the soil that compacts the seed. Learning to first sit within the vastness of it, to simply be with it, enables us to slowly release our need to find answers to those questions. Sitting in it looks so different for each griever but sit with it we must.

As we sit in it, we begin to grow comfortable with holding our love for them in new ways. If we allow ourselves, we can channel that love into others, such as I try to do with our children; loving them in ways that are much deeper. Often, I think of Duncan's big heart for those who are hurting or lost, and how he would find ways to step in. Like the time he gave a homeless man a tent from the trunk of his car to provide a moment of comfort from the elements. Finding ways to emulate this care and concern is a great way to connect and let my love for him find purpose again. Sometimes, there is simply no energy to find a place for our love, and we simply need to rest, to sit with it quietly.

Learning to first sit within the vastness of grief, to simply be with it, enables us to slowly release our need to find answers to the many questions. As we sit in it, we begin to grow comfortable with holding our love for them in new ways. If we allow ourselves, we can channel that love into others, or into actively looking for the beauty around us – and we can connect to them with the love we offer or the beauty surrounding us.

Your Light

Fearless,
brave,
and strong.
You carried so much.
You gave so much.
You were devoted,
kind,
and loyal.
You were funny.
You were smart.
You were thoughtful.
Your smile,
your laugh,
your touch,
filled so many hearts.
Your energy,
oh, your beautiful energy,
made others feel at home,
at peace,
regulated.
Of course you were human.
Of course there were faults.
But in truth,
those pale when placed next to WHO you were.
When the Darkness came for you,
it was quick,
it was loud,
it was unrelenting.
It stole all your beautiful light.

It filled your head with distortions.
It was too fierce,
even for the truths you believed with your whole being.
You were caught off guard.
Damn the Darkness
for stealing such a LIGHT.
You were indeed a light for so many.
We will seek your light.
We will remember your light.
For that was indeed who YOU, Duncan Boggess McBogg, were.
A light to remind us of our own goodness.
I love you my beloved husband, friend, and father of our boys.

June 11, 2022

Impossible

Once upon a time,
I was lost.
And my darling,
you found me
and helped me find myself.
Then,
you got lost.
And try as hard as I could,
I could not help you find your way back to you.

Sure, I did for earlier versions of you.
But, in the end,
when it mattered most,
you were stolen.

You were kidnapped by the darkness.

It was too loud
and you were blinded.
You stopped seeing us,
all of us,
even yourself.
Damn the darkness
for stealing your light!

For making it impossible to help you find your way back.

In moments of grief,
I feel I failed you.
I couldn't hold you up.

I couldn't wrap myself around what was happening.

The darkness overwhelmed you
and it confused me.
I didn't know up from down.
I just saw you disappearing,
slipping away
before my very eyes.

And I could do nothing.

I was helpless.

It was an impossible situation.

Oh,
that I could find you now,
that I could wrap my arms around you,
that I could hold you
and whisper to you all the amazing things that you are.

Yes, present tense.

You ARE.

Because you will never cease to be.

You,
your stories,
our stories,
our babies,
you still exist.
We will find our way to you.

Always loving you!

June 14, 2022

Silent Screams

Silent screams
Into pressed palms
Rivers flow
Down cheeks
And into pillows
Rocking, rocking
Cradling myself
Arms wrapped
Around
Myself
My pillow
Hands move
Wiping tears
Caressing my hair
As if comforting a child
Rocking, Rocking
Feet dangle off the edge
Mind racing
Humming with thoughts
Flashes
Memories
Both Beautiful
And fierce
Rocking, Rocking
Aching for you
For your touch
For the smell of your breath
For your arms wrapping me
For your wisdom

Your comfort
Head in hand
The rivers steadily releasing
Chest tight
Throat in knots
Breath held
And released
Rocking, Rocking
Strange sounds come forth
Caressing my hair
Cradling my face
In the crook of my hand
Silently I weep
My body longs for you
My soul cries for you
I need the safety of you
So lonely for you
My mind can't comprehend
Won't comprehend
Reliving your end
And I vanish
I disappear in my fear
Helpless
Afraid
Lost
Slipping from my grasp
You disappear
Rocking to writhing
Wounded heart cries out
Come back to me
Come

Please come
I miss you so
Drowning in my tears
They carry me
To you

July 7, 2022

The breaking of my seed's coat, my decomposition – occurred as I began to process memories and lived experiences. It was important to endure the moments when grief resulted in the examination and release of my outer coat. Allowing tears and raw honesty with my emotions, opened me to the shock of where I am planted. Sharing my innermost struggles opens me to be seen and witnessed, cracking open of my inner self, slowly creating space for the absorption necessary to grow around my grief.

SECTION TWO

EMERGENCE:
IMBIBITION AND RESPIRATION

Story of a Seed: Part Two

The rainy season began, and the seed could feel the comfort of the moisture, causing its insides to expand and the seed sat in curious dismay as the activation within caused memories to grow and swirl about. The cells within the coat began to swell and the coat began to feel tight and restrictive. It could hear the pulsing of emotions: regret, grief, and fear were in a violent war with hope, belief, and purpose. Wanting the expansion to stop, "What If?" the seed cried out into the darkness. "What if I cannot grow from this? What if I am stuck in the dark until I disappear?"

Amid its self-pity and fear, a faint glow and warmth came from above. The sun was shining down, it had heard the seeds cry and it whispered, "It's okay! You can grow!" The seed paused, becoming aware that it was not alone. "The rain and I will help you become what you are meant to be. Don't be afraid of the process, it hurts, but we will grow through it together!"

The seed scoffed, "It's too painful!" Feeling the fears grow louder, "I'm not sure I can or if I even want to do this. It hurts too much. I'm not sure I am made to grow. I am not sure I have what it takes."

"Don't give up! Keep going!" The sun was gentle in its reassurance. "This season will pass. It always does."

The seed longed for the sun to be right, but fear and grief, memories imprinted from its mother plant were strong within its core. The inner battle continued, where it came from versus where it had the potential to go. It felt safer to remain inside its coat, buried deep within the soil.

The seed could hear the creaking of its own expansion with every rainstorm and could feel the swelling in its chest grow within the warmth of the sun's light. The potential that existed within cried out in impatience, "I want to be realized!"

Then, the storm clouds rolled in, and the sun was hidden for days. The winter came and the snow began to fall. The seed felt so cold, so desperate to feel the warmth of the sun. Instead, the cold snowy blanket began to freeze the seed and wintering began. Deep within the soil, the seed could no longer see anything but darkness. The memories and imprinted experiences grew loud. The seed couldn't feel its coat expanding, in fact, it heard new sounds, sounds of withering and shrinking. The seed was becoming smaller as the darkness continued day after day. The stories inside grew louder and louder, chasing away the hope the sun had brought.

Our dear seed was now utterly lost within old scary stories and was now creating new ones, but not hopeful ones. These stories were filled with made up scenarios and distortions of past events. The seed began to feel as if the dark soil that surrounded was eating it alive.

"Without the mother plant to protect us, we will surely die down here," the thoughts grew louder with each snowstorm. The seed began to feel as if it were dying and had nearly convinced itself it was.

But the sun did return, and the thaw began. "I'm here!" The soft and gentle call of the sun came through the dark soil and began to awaken parts the seed had forgotten lived inside its coat.

Memories of knowledge passed on by the mother plant began to echo inside, "Self-compassion dear one, you are a seed and will feel the impact of the earth surrounding you, just as I did. And remember what I became, a beautiful plant, that bore fruit, that brought you into existence. This potential lives inside you too. It is who you are. You are made to grow and bear fruit." The seed breathed in this intrinsic wisdom and felt the fear of death fade a bit and was caught off guard by the return of inner swelling. Down the edges of its coat, the swelling grew, it wanted to break free and experience and partake of the nutrients that surrounded it. Instinctively, the seed began to relax a bit with the knowledge the mother had instilled deep within.

As the tiny root began to break the barrier of the coat, the seed was exhilarated by the changes it felt. It was beginning to grow into its truth. It could hear the words of the mother living within, "You were made for this." The energy brought forth by the sun and the deep inner wisdom propelled the tiny root and branched it out in every direction, growing it. The excitement the seed felt impacted each grain of soil it encountered. After some resistance, the soil gave way, allowing the roots to grow far and wide. The soil was happy to welcome this new visitor and nourished it with a nutrient-dense embrace.

The Process

As we settle into the soil, and the seed of our new self begins to adjust, we can begin to crack. The cracking allows us to absorb and expand. We begin the process of imbibition, where absorption drives respiration, creating structural changes and expansion. Our dormant season allows the environment we are planted in to slowly transform us. As we absorb the impact of our loss, what lies within us is stirred. Courageously stepping into each day allows moisture and the pressures around us to erode and crack open our coats. We begin to change ever so slowly, and our storytelling and protective parts begin to seek a different sort of survival. We are preparing for something new, to grow differently than the former plant of self, from which this new seed was created.

I have learned in my three years as a suicide-loss survivor and during a brief stint as a student of counseling, the importance of self-care, social support, self-disclosure, and self-compassion for posttraumatic growth. Feeling safe is often one of the most difficult aspects faced in stigmatized loss. Feeling safe with others, within ourselves, and within the world can feel daunting and impossible as waves of grief overtake us. Sitting with our stories, our emotions, and feelings, while truly allowing ourselves to surrender to the experience of them often feels terrifying and unsafe. Yet, it is so necessary to do as we heal. Doing this in small doses as our nervous system allows, often with the guidance of an empathetic professional, can help set us on a path toward healing. We cannot rush this process.

Finding safe spaces in which connection and belonging are there to support us on this journey allows us to open and share what is on our hearts. This vulnerability paves the pathway for common threads to be found while dissolving isolation and loneliness. We begin to see where our "parts" are rooted in distortions. Shame, guilt, and judgments can begin to soften their grip, while fear and anxiety can be nurtured back toward safety. In sharing our struggles openly, we begin to weave the threads of community and our connection to the greater whole begins to strengthen as we find grace for others who are also struggling and as others embrace us in our struggles. Compassion is where the very nature of being human can be witnessed and accepted, this is where healing begins. Compassion does not just come from the external, it also must be found within self. This is where the structural changes of respiration occur, where we begin to allow ourselves to expand and grow, where our primary root begins to sprout and push its way down into the soil. The resistance met while pressing down creates a strength that could easily be overlooked, but it is so vital to the upward growth which follows.

The process of emergence is vastly different for each griever. Each of us are planted in different environments and our seed was created from different plants, under very different circumstances. My process will be different from yours, which will vary from all the grievers we encounter. Our propensity to crack open and our resilience is impacted by so many factors. For me, the need for safety was met as I was surrounded by the warmth and light of friends witnessing and watering me with their grace and acceptance, sharing their stories and carrying me through when I could not find my footing. It was found as friends sat with me, walked me through anniversaries, and held my hand when the loneliness threatened to swallow me whole. It came from friends who made themselves available at all moments, day or night – a phone call away. It came as I wept with them, relived stories and memories with them, and when they were unafraid to say his name. It came as I spoke what was scary and vomited my dark thoughts and fears upon them, and they remained unflinchingly by my side, reminding me of what is true. It came in creating new traditions and getting out into nature with them on long walks or hikes.

As we are working toward this safety, we must find spaces to just be. It is too much to be continually working on and processing our grief and all that it brings to the surface. There is great peace found in balance. To find balance, connecting with our physical environment can offer us healing as well. Nature itself offers so many great examples of life and the cycles therein: birth, growth, beauty, inter-dependence, aging, rest and dormant seasons, regeneration and so the cycle goes. Each aspect of nature depends on the others to do their part. As the seed grows and creates food or shelter, creatures feast and find safety, and they in turn live and create balance among themselves. The wind presses on the tree creating strength in the resistance. While each element and organism help sustain another, we too can learn to help others with the fruits produced by our hardships and joys.

As nature offers us balance, so does pouring ourselves into others. Finding moments of joy and laughter as we remember our grief does not define us. The dark soil we are planted in does not define us, it is a container in which we grow. It nurtures us and offers us the opportunity to crack open, absorb, and change. It allows us to sprout and grow a primary root that will hold us fast and provide nutrients as we begin to grow. These next poems are about the process of absorption, structural changes, and growing a primary root.

A Log and a Line

I surrender.
I lay back, arms wide,
and I allow this river to take me.
Why?
Because I've reached the falls.
I've learned along the way
that fighting the mighty river leaves you weary,
overtaken,
nearly drowned,
and incapable of moving to safety.
I know to fight it is certain death.
The mighty river ebbs and flows.
And after a long winter,
it rages.
Our river rages.
Knocking me a bit like a rag doll,
I am battered and bruised,
I can no longer fight it.
Friends throw branches and safety lines.
When I can,
I grab them for reprieve.
I rest a moment
until the next wave comes to carry me away again.
The wave of your passing has left me stunned,
dazed,
lost.
Now, a second wave comes.
A diagnosis,
a rare disease

visits me,
knocking me a good one.
I see now I have little control.
I'm at the bottom of this waterfall.
All I can do is lay back,
arms wide,
floating in surrender.
I give.
Oh, mighty river,
you have my attention –
though it is filled with weary exhaustion.
I dare not ask for a rest.
Though admittedly,
I long for a break.
I long for fall to arrive.
The current to calm.
I long for winter to freeze the water
so, I can be carried off to the warmth.
I am so weary worn.
The good news is I like to float,
until then, float I will.
Praying the river will calm.
Praying a lifeline comes before the winter storms.

September 11, 2021

Foggy Visitation

You came with the fog.
Gently at first.
The reminder of you growing as I sat in it.
A drive to the place you loved most,
but I didn't make it.
Stopping short,
I wept.
You flooded me and I became angry.
You created a norm.
You made the unthinkable, thinkable.
And the pieces of you,
now vulnerable,
stir my fury.
Endless questioning,
I defer to understanding and the need to survive.
Walking.
Aimless.

November 4, 2021

Grief Experienced

Have you ever found yourself in grief?
In a moment when tears fall
and angry questions swirl in a flurry in your mind?
And you scream,
but the scream comes from so deep within that it is silent.
A silent and brutally visceral sound.
A sound that is long
and crinkles your face into a contorted mess as one comes out
after the next?
All the while your mind explodes with so much sorrow that when
you finish,
you just have a numb humming sensation throughout your
being?
Then, you sit silently before the next wave hits
and you start all over with the thoughts of anger and sorrow.
Questioning everything,
literally everything.
When you watch your beloved suffer,
falling apart before your eyes
and you are literally helpless to stop it,
something changes inside you.
You are no longer the same.
Something breaks inside of you,
trauma enters.
You not only grieve their death,
but the death of the beautiful memories.
Because the struggle,
the hurt,
the pain,

replaces them.
You have to sit in the numbness until your system can process it,
or so I'm told.
I've also been promised that the numbness will thaw.
"It really will," they say,
"It's there to protect you," they continue.
I want to be reassured,
but in truth, I'm not.
Grief is forever.
Every new stage my babies will enter
is guaranteed to usher in a new wave to navigate.
Every new choice or decision I make
will do the same.
I f*%#@!* miss you, my love!
How the hell am I supposed to do this without you?
We all miss you,
our best friend,
father,
and love of my life.

December 4, 2021

Overwhelming waves of emotions flood grievers. The range is so wide, and each one is essential to process, often repeatedly and over many years. Grievers gain the ability to predict which ones will come given certain circumstances and learn to navigate them. In early grief however, these waves feel unpredictable and unsettling. Many grievers come to the same words to describe this feeling; untethered and homeless are the ones I came to early in my grief. I felt a huge sense of comfort when I found other grievers used these very words, I felt I was not alone in this journey – though I was deeply burdened at the enormity of humans who experience this. I have come to a deep understanding that grief truly goes hand in hand with love. The range of emotions, though felt and expressed in a thousand different ways, is beginning to appear like a universal truth, an experience no living soul can escape this life without.

Processing these many emotions is part of the absorption phase in the germination of grief. I was planted in soil that was dark and scary, while still feeling the warmth of loving friends and family. I was cradled in the coldest season of my life, and I experienced a sensation of being numb to the reality of the feelings and emotions that arose. I knew that while I had moments when my outer coat allowed the raw truths to enter through the cracks forming, I also had the shelter of my protective parts numbing the experience to allow me to only process what I could handle in those early months. I could rock into the pain for a short moment, then retreat out into the warmth the sun filled the surrounding soil with, allowing me a moments rest before another wave came.

The trauma of watching a beloved suffer leaves an indelible mark, one that will seep back into consciousness as grief progresses. Memories and flashes will come – it's a guarantee. But this is where the beauty of our nervous system plays such an incredible role in protecting us. It allows in just enough to begin absorbing and ushers us back out in an act of survival. Healing is a slow process for many who experience stigmatized losses because much of what we saw and experienced was overwhelming to our systems. There is freedom found in embracing with self-compassion, the fact that there is no timetable for our grief.

Longing

In the wind,
I feel you near,
There is a calm,
to ease my fear.
As the hawk comes flying in,
riding invisible waves,
reflecting on my tears.

Missing you every second.
My mind drifts,
my cells cry out,
my body, longing,
carrying grief,
pain,
shame.

My love,
I miss your magic,
your presence,
the comfort of our connection.

January 8, 2022

Untethered

I read this word today in relation to grief.

Untethered.

That absolutely fits.

It's like I'm always free falling now.
Like the world has become this endless vacuum,
where I'm being sucked in.
I am missing the one thing that held me steady, my soulmate.
Some days it's a blind free fall,
others, it's like I'm suspended in time and space, everything in
slow-motion.
But always, there is this Untethered feeling.

My soul,
My very being was tied to my love.
Now that he is gone,
I'm Untethered.

January 30, 2022

At Your Grave

Talking,
weeping,
leaving messages in the snow,
I'm reminded
you asked me to marry you on Valentine's Day.
In my apartment,
you scared me.
You acted weird.
Then got on your knee,
impulsive like you'd do.
You asked me to marry you.
You only had your silver ring,
you placed it on my finger.
I said yes!
Immediately,
I knew.
From the second you chose me,
you respected me.
You were utterly safe.
You were the only one I ever felt
completely safe with.
You carried my secrets,
my wounds,
You carried me
with love,
always.

I miss you so much!

February 14, 2022

There is no way out of this....

Life is moving on,
I am not.
I am stuck.
Being stuck is not new to me
as I have been stuck for the past many years.
But this stuck,
the stuck without you,
I can't really process it.
Nine months in
And the icy edges are thawing.
I am feeling.
I am not distracted.
I am stuck in it.
Every fiber of my being
sticks to memories of you,
sits with absolute discomfort,
loneliness,
fear.
Loss of where I belong.
I do not belong anymore.
I gave you my heart
and you gave me yours.
We gave ourselves to each other.
Yet, you tore yourself away.
Something inside of you broke
and you impulsively chose not to wait.
I was trying to find a way.
I was trying to find a different means of help.
You didn't give me enough time.

I couldn't process
Any
Of
It!
You hurt me.
You hurt us.
You were hurting.
Dying did not make it better,
it made it all worse.
I'd rather you were still here
than to have you die alone.
Oh honey,
You died without me by your side.
I wish I could have held you at least.
I had been so torn
between helping you
and protecting the boys.
God,
I wish I could have held you.
I wish I had slowed down
and BEEN WITH you.
My trauma response is to get busy.
So, I got busy.
I should have spent that time
sitting with you,
holding you,
listening to you,
validating you.
Oh, my love,
I am so sorry!
I am sorry this perfect storm swept over all of us.

I want to hold you
right now!
I want to tell you how much I love you.
I want to tell you how much you mean to me.
I want to tell you that I am who I am because of you.
You were my everything.
You were my only safe place.
Now, I am so scared,
so alone,
so vulnerable.
Any strength you saw
Was because you were at my side.
How could you have left us?
How could you have stopped seeing the boys?
How?
What happened to you?
What if you had something else going on?
Honey!!!!!
God, what if you had a brain tumor?
I want you here.
I am so lost without you.
The best part of me is gone.
You were the best person for me.
You were made for me.
I wish I could have done something differently.
I wish I could have changed this story.

February 18, 2022

Structural changes come as the thawing begins and absorption progresses, often the questions increase. "What ifs" and the "shoulds" come in with a ferocity one cannot fight easily. Here it is often the support of good friends who pull us out and help us to see reason. There are times when we wisely know these inquiries are simply our mind attempting to rewrite an unalterable storyline. In cases of addiction and suicide, loss survivors often wrestle with the experience of powerlessness. It feels nearly impossible at times to accept the loss was beyond our control. We loved them, so why was our love not enough to give us the right words, the strength, or the wisdom to have changed this outcome.

This internal wrestling for me was and sometimes returns as a fierce and very loud accusatory part. It is so difficult to see even this part arrives to protect. This part wants to change an unchangeable outcome, and we must hold its hand and walk with it as a child. We must speak with gentleness, helping to bring understanding that it was not our fault. This child part of us is hurting and in desperate need of self-compassion. When we cannot muster compassion for ourselves, finding loving helpers along our journey is an absolute necessity for our survival.

Advice

Love on them
Always
Every second
Tell them
Speak it
Pay attention
Listen
Listen not just to what they say
But also, to what they don't
Listen to their body
Listen to their spirit
Listen to their silence
Their solitude
When you hear
Act
Ask
Inquire
Stop
Sit
Clasp hands
Hug
Hold
Presence
Let your hearts connect
Gaze into each other's eyes
And hold it
Hold space
Breathe together
'til the rhythm is in time

Make music of the moment
Now
Always
Forever
Together as one

February 21, 2022

F%#!

Fuck!
Fuck!
Fuckity fuck!!!
I miss you!
But only as much as my system allows.
I can't process this.
I can't fathom this.

I'm trying to move in the direction this river has me on,
but it's unsteady,
it's fierce,
it digs into the heart of me,
challenging my very identity.
Not only am I untethered from you,
I am seeing how much of my identity was in you.
Because of you.
I had you always.
And in you I was safe.
You let yourself be my home.

Now, a homeless wanderer,
I misstep,
I fall,
I struggle,
I disappear.

Finding my way
to myself,
I've been lost a while –

even before you left me.
I have been on this journey all my life.
You were a help mate,
a guide.
I fucking miss you!
No one gets me in the way you did.

May 2, 2022

Imagine

It's empty.
No one is there.
Just a stack of pillows
that once cradled his head.
A nightstand
with his stuff still in the drawers.
Even the dog can't stand the loneliness of it tonight
and has curled up at my feet.

Sometimes,
I imagine him there.
I imagine rolling on my side
having chats about our boys,
Holding his hand when a nightmare attacks,
laughing at his snores.

I imagine him watching his show, Cobra Kai,
with headphones in
so I don't have to hear the ridiculousness.
And putting my head on his shoulder, watching the kick-assery
anyway,
in silence,
giving him shit,
laughing together.

I imagine what we'd be arguing about these days,
discussing intensely,
shaking our head at the state of the world.

Wondering together about the future for our boys.
I imagine his advice as he calmed an anxious moment.

But mostly,
I imagine his arms encircling me,
holding me safe,
calming me,
being my home.

June 23, 2022

Late Night Ramble

My shadow misses your shadow,
my head, that shoulder,
my hands, those hands.
My knee misses knocking into your knee.
My eyes miss viewing what you too, are seeing.
My heart misses all of you.
I need you, my love.
I don't feel like being strong.
I'm so damn tired from carrying what we once shared.
It still doesn't make sense,
it likely never will.
I know this.
I know I have no choice but to learn to live alongside my grief.
I suppose I am, with each step.
But those steps feel heavy with the muck of grief.
Last year at this time I was able to see beauty in the world,
to be entranced by the birds and the nature that surrounds.
This year, I live the cautionary warnings that the 2nd year is the
most difficult.
It has been so far.
I feel the loss of you so much more profoundly.
The supports are falling away.
My steps creating a new path.
My loneliness grows.
I cannot fathom filling that space with another.
I cannot imagine ever being known as deeply by another.
You walked with me through defining moments,
moments that were ours alone.
Weeks after you died
it was callously asked of me if I would remarry –

I'm so "young after all."
That question still bothers me.
It was too soon.
Sixteen months later,
and it's still too soon.
You are irreplaceable.
Could I find love again someday?
Sure, I'm an open and vulnerable human who values connection,
but I curiously sit in my loneliness as it's what remains of you.
That loneliness, though so incredibly painful, is my connection to
you.
It visits me throughout the day.
It's where you would be.
My loneliness is what I have that actively IS you.
I need to make friends with it.
Perhaps that is why I don't sleep well?
It's most present at night.
I somehow need it
because I need you.
I have not let you go.
I don't want to.
My loneliness grows
because my love for you shows up as my loneliness.
Where do I place the love that belongs only to you?
It defaults to my loneliness,
this is love lost.
When I have the mind to
I will rechannel it.
For now,
I will be with it until sleep finds me.

October 24, 2022

There are moments when the loneliness becomes all-consuming and swallows the grieving widow whole. When the darkness of the soil that surrounds feels so bleak and cold and self-care gets lost entirely. The desire to crawl out of bed and join a world without our person disappears and the warrior within us grows wisely silent. There is a strange comfort in being with the loneliness, for it is a space where our spirit sits with theirs and we grieve the loss of them. It is a sacred space and is as important as connecting with the outside world.

It is here where we feel the loss and allow it to reside. It is here where the reality settles in and our tears, if we allow them, release the regrets and longings held deeply within. It is here where healing on a soul level, healing with our person in private conversations, a newfound intimacy with the lost one, can begin to guide our mind into our present truth. We must summon our warrior spirit and throw our legs over the edge of our beds and rise to our feet. We must rise because the world outside beckons to us, like the sun, speaking supportive words and encouraging us to reengage and continue our own growth. We also must grow down into the soil by creating roots first, and this is done as we absorb the reality we face without our beloved. We must contend with their loss, and we must find ways to make peace with them. This will look so different for each one of us.

The Road

I never imagined
this road would be a lonely one,
as I had you by my side.
With you there
I knew I could face anything that came.
Now that you were stolen away,
the load we shared
falls squarely upon my shoulders.
I'm now bent,
as a crone,
under the weight.
It's crushing my quickly aging bones.
I can but crawl and claw my way along,
stopping on occasion
when the sun shines on me.
Resting in feline repose for that singular moment,
'til the clouds thunder back in
and the rains weigh the load I carry.
I try,
yes, I try to grasp the youthful apple.
To take a bite
with hope that it will give life to my shriveling soul.
There must be hope,
this brokenness can't be all that remains.

October 29, 2022

Grief Theater

In the dark
The hum
The ache
The quickening
Ignites
Behind the curtain
Stories dance around
Waiting to be remembered
Awareness
Alive
But not
Memories
Not new creations
These Stories of the past
Intertwine
Peeking through the curtain
To see if the audience awaits
Tugged back in by an eager past
Ready to comingle with imagined wishes
Twirling the memory around
Til in a dizzying display
It sprouts anew
Not real
Not false
Just a dream to break through
Bursting the curtains wide
The stage bursts to life
In a nonsensical rhythm
The tale confounds with its semi-truths

It's bedeviled illusions
Distorted fragments
Hidden by fog
By shadow
Backlit by the ever-judging eye of the director
Who is often overtaken by the frenetic dance of past and present
desire
And all become weightless
The stage growing distant
Further and further
Til the context is lost
Til the imagery fades
And the dancers now mere impressions
Yet their mobility remains
In silent, invisible
Experiential
Dimensions
And a new audience awakens
Infantile
In need
In presence

In presence

It absorbs
Consumes

October 30, 2022

Bereaved Hallucinations

I can still conjure the feeling of you.
I can still feel what it felt when I could call on you.
I can still sense what it would have felt like when you were near.
When I'm driving in my car and lost in thought,
I can still feel the feelings of you,
the comfort of you,
the safety of you.
But then it all crashes down in an instant
when truth reminds me that you're gone.
I don't always know what to do with this feeling –
it just keeps going in,
coming and going.
I feel so lost without you.
Life has a funny way
when you've lost the one you love,
of reminding you at every corner what you've lost.
Unrelenting,
Unfriendly,
and unkind at moments,
at other moments
it is beautiful and kind.
Sometimes life bestows upon you the shadow of His wings,
where you have a moment of memory that brings a smile to your
face.

November 11, 2022

When the Darkness Came

I was who I was
because your love lifted me up.
It carried me
in safety.
It held me,
supported me,
and comforted me
in the warmth of your arms.
I knew I was never alone.
I was cherished.
I was yours,
body and soul.
I could grow,
fall down,
get lost,
and your hand was always there.
Always.

Until,
the darkness came.
Where it was born,
where it came from exactly,
I'm uncertain.
My mind continually makes stories to explain.

Genetics?
The demons of your father?
Your past?

My misplaced words?
Society?

Lies filled your mind with distortions,
sneaky and subtle.
At first
confusing,
confounding,
weakening you,
slowly poisoning your beautiful spirit.
Over time,
but for how long?
Your lifetime?
They stole your sleep
then they put out your light.
Evil bastards!
They took your fire,
your strength,
your fight.
They blinded you to who you were,
to me,
to us,
to our babies,
to the very fact that you were –
are –
in fact,
loved immensely.

You will forever and always
be loved.

Wherever your spirit resides,
I hope you see,
I hope you can rest now,
in the knowledge
that you continue to be loved.

June 3, 2023

Second Year Reflections

Two years ago
my beloved lost his battle against the darkness that comes for some.
I don't want to dwell on that
because that was not who HE was.
He was kind.
He was compassionate .
He was loving.
He adored his children
and cherished me.
He worked so hard...so, so hard
to provide for us.
He was
a son,
a friend,
a father,
a husband,
a leader,
a curious discoverer,
an adventurer,
a gymnast,
a coach,
a classroom engineer,
a camping enthusiast,
a researcher,
a dog lover,
a dreamer,
a mountain man,
a daredevil,
a media fanatic,
a news junkie,

a fierce protector,
an activist,
a political guru (seriously, you could ask him anything, and he
knew every backstory),
a teacher,
I could go on and on...

Mostly, he was my best friend.
I miss him every second of the day.
My entire being,
even my cells (I swear I feel it),
long for him.

Duncan, wherever your spirit flies,
I hope you feel all the love we carry in our souls for you.
You are forever loved,
deeply missed,
and eternally ours.

Friends, get out there today and love on your people.
Let the stupid shit go.
Fight for those too tired to fight anymore.
Stop being afraid to ask for help when you truly need it.

Spend a moment in nature today.
And if you see a hawk,
it just might be my Duncan
nodding down at you.

Love you!

June 10, 2023

Liminal Spaces

There are liminal spaces in grief
where life throws you into very lonely places.
You are no longer part of the world around you
or
part of the life you once had.
You now sit in the space in-between.
You must walk this place alone.
There is not a soul who fully understands your unique experience,
for it is truly unique to you.

August 1, 2023

Part of expansion in grief involves contending with difficult realities that now exist. For me, the realization about how much this experience is as unique to me as our relationship was, felt very lonely. Knowing others understood the fundamentals of grief, had experienced many of the same emotions and wrestled with similar themes as I was, felt simultaneously comforting and confusing. I relied on the stories of others to guide me and bring me hope, and I still find solace in the fact that I am not alone. However, there are these spaces in grief where the everyday nuances which belonged to both Duncan and I alone, are now missing. These spaces require me to sit with them, to continue a relationship with a person whose physical form no longer dwells with me, but whose spirit lingers. These liminal spaces are ours alone, each griever carries their own spaces created with their person. Accepting these in-between spaces has allowed me to walk with a little more ease in my day to day.

As we process all of this, grief also scratches old wounds, re-exposing them. There comes a time for many of us where the wounds from our childhood make an appearance and we find ourselves doubled over in the heaviness. Our past wounds often created similar marks on our souls and if they were unhealed, they may begin to beg for attention as our nervous systems sense the familiarity and want to protect us. This part of grief takes so many grievers by surprise; however, it is a very common experience. Our protective parts are on high alert and remember.

Feel It

Grief did not enter when my love died.
It entered before I could speak.
It came when I had no concept of what it was.
A soul wound from a protector.
I grew up feeling separate,
different.
It came again, more obviously,
when a beloved pet ran away.
And again, at the loss of my great grandmother.
It revisited when a dear friend died
and
once more at the passing of my grandpa,
lost babies,
the suicide of my father-in-law,
then my granny's death.

Grief also came in the form of lost friendships,
romantic relationships,
loss of innocence,
and ideals,
loss of faith,
and belief in goodness,
family secrets,
and loss of home,
safety,
and humanities inability to care for others.

Grief has always been there
in its various forms.
It is part of me.

But it is with the loss of my love that I see it fully.

I see it more deeply.

I finally feel it,
As opposed to only walking with it.

November 16, 2023

Being Seen

I miss the way you saw me.
There are times I wonder if anyone will ever truly see me again?
You introduced me to myself.
You cracked my world wide open.
You showed me what love is,
and even now,
you are teaching me still.

If I close my eyes and conjure you,
there is a feeling of home,
comfort,
rest,
and safety.

I would choose you all over again –
even knowing this ending.

November 28, 2023

Being seen begins to feel like a luxury when you spend much of your days inside your mind processing and doing the work of grief. When you are fortunate enough to find others who not only see you but witness your reality, it is a balm on your soul. For so many of us, the loss of our beloved stole away a place of safety and comfort, of complete acceptance. Grappling with this loss means we must find safety within ourselves; yet the exuberant joy of finding safety with another allows our systems to relax into healing. It tells our system we are not alone in this journey and there are others who will walk this road with us. As we begin to open ourselves up this safety begins to feel palpable and real, however it often comes on the heels of a season buried deep in the soil – of reflecting and facing so many fears.

SECTION THREE

SELF-SUPPORTING: RESERVES

Story of a Seed: Part Three

One day, when the seed was gaining confidence and feeling stronger, the sun whispered, "I feel a storm coming, please hold fast. I am always here, and you will feel me again soon" and then disappeared behind a cloud.

The earth grew cold as the moments passed and the shivering seed cried out, "But I thought it was time to grow? I was ready. I thought it was time!" The old familiar fears crept in and gave birth to new ones.

"The mother plant was not what you thought. It was not as strong as you had supposed," came a raspy detractor. "You came from something that was not as it appeared. It was all a lie." The seed felt an intensity within its coat that it had not yet encountered and began to tremble, doubting the knowledge within its coat. It sat in the soil stunned and confused, fully aware of its newly grown roots.

"What do you know is true?" the soil asked, feeling the anxious thoughts of the seed vibrating through its roots.

The seed's thoughts were interrupted by this question. "What is true?" This question brought forth the power to silence the loud voice of the detractor, and the seed began to muster the courage to combat the lies. The seed sat with the discomfort inside its coat and simply listened, straining to hear the other voices within. "What do I know is true?"

"We cannot control the weather, but we understand the ebb and flow." This gentle message came from a place somewhere deep inside, a place that felt like the Mother. Peace and calm filled the seed, and it knew, "Just rest for a spell."

For the first time since it had found its way to the ground, the seed knew, from the depth of its core, it would become something. It was unsure of how much of a thing it would become, but the knowing brought purpose. So, it listened to the inner wisdom, and rested while waiting out the storm. It felt nice to rest. It was in the resting where the seed began to realize how much it had been working. The seed saw for the first time the ways in which its journey may have made it stronger. The ways in which the belly of the grackle impacted its coat, preparing it for its journey in the soil. How the excrement became nutrients upon which its roots were now feeding. How the very cold and dark soil were protecting it from washing away, giving it a safe home. Something was changing inside the seed. The voice of the mother plant, imprinted deep within its core, began to spring forth in spontaneous knowing. And for a glorious while, our seed rested in the darkness before the next visitor made an appearance.

"You think you know so much?" came a new voice, the voice of self-doubt. "How do you know you will become something? Perhaps all you will be is a tiny sprout which will wither in the sun?" The voice did not stop, and as it noticed it had the seed's attention continued to spiral on, "You may get trampled by the animals that pass by? Eaten by a slug? You may catch a disease and die!" It repeated, "How do you know you are to become something? Perhaps you will be lost like so many other seedlings before you, only to wither away?"

"Whoa!" cried the seed. "Could all of that really happen? Is that what awaits me if I grow? Is it safer to stay down here?" The racing of potential dangers began to course throughout the insides of this tiny coat. The seed felt it surely should stop growing and shrink back within itself, where it was safe – where it knew itself. The seed sat, frozen with self-doubt.

Moisture began to fill the soil as the rains began. It began to speak to the seed in low and soft tones, "Drink dear one, my waters tell a different story. Listen." The seed quieted doubt with a "shush!"

Straining to hear, thousands of tiny voices began to whisper, "Drink." "Drink." "Drink." "Soak us in!" And drink it did! The tiny seed felt itself expanding with the nurturing rain, "You were created with a purpose."

The soil, filled with moisture, hugged the seed with reassurance, "I know you miss the mother plant. I know you long for home. I know the comforts you formed in are gone and this is all new. I know. I see you dear one. I promise, I want to be a safe place for you to grow. The sun, the rain, and I will work together for you. Try to rest again, we have you."

Unsure of its ability to trust the process, another voice from deep within the coat decided it was time to make itself known, "Span of control my dear, span of control," came a crisp and sharp voice.

"What does that mean?" The seed was trying so hard to pay attention to all the parts that kept appearing.

The thinking mind of the seed came in with its protective advice, "Span of control simply means you cannot control the forces outside of you. You can only control the way you perceive and think about the many factors coming your way." Thinking mind was rather matter of fact in its approach. "You can't even always control what is inside your coat! So, you really must learn to go with the flow. Accept what is and make the best of it." There was a dismissiveness that the seed did not like, and it did not feel comforted in the slightest.

"Are you telling me I have no control? I am at the mercy of the weather and the soil and whatever wisdom the mother plant deposited inside my coat?" The seed was not sure it appreciated this perspective. Certainly, it could control something other than its perceptions and thoughts! And really, could it control those? So many came unannounced and really tried to take over on a regular basis. "Gosh, what if I have no control whatsoever?" Now the seed was caught in a totally different battle, could it survive even its own thoughts? Oh, the despair the poor seed found itself sitting in.

And there it sat.

And sat.

And sat.

Until the rains subsided and the clouds rolled away, unveiling the sun once again.

"Why hello there my friend." The sun was cheery and seemed to be nudging the seed with its warmth.

The seed rotated slightly toward the sun, and sighed, "Oh, hey."

"Why so glum, didn't you enjoy the rain?"

The seed was tempted to stay in its depressed state, but the mention of the rain did perk its spirits a bit. It managed a pretend enthusiasm, "It was nice." The seed wasn't really feeling it, but knew it was true.

"Now that the rain has saturated you, I can warm you up a bit. I think you might be surprised by how you feel." The sun filled the soil with its warm glow and the heat began to sink deeper into the ground until it reached the seed.

It really did feel nice. The warmth began to distract the seed from all its concerns, and soon the seed felt something happening inside its coat. Something entirely new, like some other part of it was being awakened! This new part was so strong, and the seed liked the strength that was growing inside, it reminded the seed of the root growth. "I'm growing!" cried the seed in delight. "My insides feel strong in your warmth and light!"

The combination of the rain's water saturating the seed with purpose, the soils safe and encouraging, nutrient rich hug, and the suns loving warmth and light caused all the potential that lay deep inside the seeds coat to expand. The expansion pressed upwards trying to get to the sun, it wanted to see the sun, to feel it outside the protection of the soil. It wanted to hear more clearly the wisdom of the sun.

The Process

Grief shows up so differently for each of us, as we bring to it our own stories. We see what has occurred through a veil of previous experiences and our capacity to sit with it varies widely. Resiliency looks different from one individual to the next, and it is so imperative that we do not compare our situation and reactions to anyone else's. When we think of becoming self-supported, it hinges heavily upon what exists within our "seed." What do we enter this grief journey with? What knowledge did we gain along the way? What tools have we previously developed to help us through difficulty? What is our capacity toward self-acceptance? Do we understand our own span of control? Are our relationships stable and supportive? In the end, the real question becomes, do these old resources continue to work? Can I stand in the midst of this devastation?

In the soil, as we begin to absorb and crack open, we are still in the darkness. We are still in a period of introspection and while the outside world is seeping into the soil, watering us and the sunlight trying hard to warm us, our growth is one of personal understanding and contending with where we find ourselves as new roots begin to form. During this time, our self-talk and the stories we have grown so accustomed to dance about in our minds. We begin to feel the respiration – the cellular changes that are happening inside us. This can be a scary time, because sometimes our entire identity is shaken. Who am I now? How does who I was mesh with this new soil in which I find myself? Where I once needed the warmth of friendships and relationships to grow, I may now find the cold preferable. Where I once was quenched by the waters of wisdom, I may now find myself overwhelmed and incapable of absorbing it. Those who felt safe, may now perplex us. All that held us may seem to have new meaning and we often no longer know what to do within ourselves. We are thrown into a place that requires us to feel everything to its fullness. This does not just mean the event of the loss itself, but all the things it stirs up inside of us.

As a child, I was never shown how to handle my big feelings, I had to learn how this was done on my own. Because of this, I developed coping mechanisms that worked for my younger self, but now as a middle-aged woman, they wreak havoc on my inner peace. Hypervigilance is my go-to when I feel unsafe, and make no mistake, losing your spouse to suicide feels very unsafe. Suddenly, the one person who I felt the safest with is gone in such an unfathomable manner. The one person who knew me inside and out and still chose to love me, chose to leave not only me, but life itself. He left our children too. One of the most difficult aspects of grappling with suicide-loss is to gather all the wisdom I have harnessed and apply it to my life.

I have learned the safety I once found in meditation, in breathwork, and in mindful walks now evoke scary emotions and feelings within my body. The solitude required in these self-regulating methods can be very unsettling for so many. When wrestling with unprocessed feelings experienced while watching your loved one unravel; the story is relived not just in your mind, but within your body as well. Tools meant to bring you into the present moment may be perceived as a threat and create emotionally charged physiological responses. An important part of respiration is allowing ourselves the grace to set aside tools that once served us while waiting until our nervous systems are grounded enough to be able to support them once again.

It is crucial to acknowledge we are not failing when, or if, widely recognized tools no longer work as they once did. Rather, if we can compassionately embrace our nervous systems as they rely on our reserves to craft narratives based on previous experiences, embracing new realizations and sitting with feelings as they arise; allows supportive molecular changes to occur, which is integral to our healing. Accepting this, and learning to adapt to where we are planted, allows us to grow around the stories and experiences we have lived. Expanding and sprouting our new roots takes time, and that time is dependent upon each specific seed and varies with each origin story. It is in this period of germination where we find ourselves waiting, endeavoring to discover a new capacity to trust in a process we still do not understand.

Identity

I can't sleep,
my head is full of so many things.
I can't figure out which one to grab ahold of and sit with.
I need to sit with some things.
I am so completely overwhelmed, and I feel terribly lost.
Who the hell am I?
This person emerging is foreign to me.
I'm unable to feel all the feelings and identify them,
unable to set forth a thought and hold on and follow through.
Missing the hell out of my soul mate,
and feeling so completely alone.
Realizing I may never again know a man's touch,
never feel strong arms around me,
never have someone who just gets it –
just knows.
I may never again have someone who fiercely protects me,
who considers others yet remains secure in himself.

Feeling abandoned,
angry that life throws endless challenges my way.
Simultaneously feeling the connection to the greater whole,
yet so far away from it.
Continually being haunted by ghostly memories of your illness.
Til death do us part.
I don't want to part.
I want you with us.
I need you with us.
I don't trust me without us.
I don't know me without us.

I knew all the support would start to fade.
I knew only a trusted few would continue to check in.
I knew this time would come,
where it would all become so very real.
I think of you, and I get angry.
Because if you hadn't left me, I wouldn't be in this confounded
place.
I'd be safe in the comfort you provided,
I'd be home, not lost.

Somehow, I am still reaching out,
I am still living.
I celebrate our babies
and sit with them.
Yet sometimes I cannot connect,
this angers me.
It reminds me that you left us.
That some part of you chose to give up.
I get angry at the legacy you created for them.
It isn't fair.
It isn't what you wanted for them, for us.
I am so sad!
Suicide!
Fathers!
Hereditary illness and disease!
* Medications that did not help, but rather hurt!
I am reeling!

October 25, 2021

Note: Medications are necessary in many cases.

Roll Over, Get Up

In the waking hours
I reach out
As my mind awakens
To this ever-present reality
I'm without you
You are gone

I'm asked of life
To wake and move forward
To allow memories
Both joyous and painful
To co-mingle

Daily
I roll off this bed
Sometimes tear streaked and puffy
Others with bravery
With the strength one finds
In places still not understood

Life gives few choices
Choose life or not
Live wholly or as a ghost
And then I hear them

Our babies

Laughing in the other room
Footsteps coming my way

And I know

There is but one

Roll over
Get up
Be brave
Face the world
As it is

Continue in love
Wrapping arms
Holding
Crying
Laughing
Get up

Go on

November 7, 2021

The Wagging Finger

Failure,
it comes at me
screaming,
where were you?
Why did you not … ?

I feel so utterly broken.
I let you down,
in fear,
in anger,
in confusion and overwhelm –
I wasn't there.

You were disappearing,
so was I.

Where did we go?

This hole,
the walls grow steeper
as the bottom continues to drop.

I'm in darkness
and it's more than I can take.
The wagging finger,
relentless.

Occasionally,
Someone shines a light down.
I turn on my own flashlight at times

And I can see the wings that surround me.
Realizing they are mine,
I rise.

The next wave of darkness,
rushing me,
pushing me back,
deeper into the hole I tumble.

I fall,
rushing down.
No bottom in sight.
Falling.
Falling.
Momentum.
I get lost.

Tears.
Wailing.

Release.

Breath.

In and out,

in,
in,
in,

hold.

Slow exhale.

I feel them,
my wings flutter,
reflexively
they open,
slowing my free fall.

I hover.

In the darkness,
glimmers shine down from above.

I rest in them,
feeling them,
breathing into them.

I catch my breath.

Aware.

Numbness,
shock,
loneliness,
hold me in place –
neither up nor down,
just suspended.

I wait.

November 8, 2021

There comes a time for so many grievers when we become aware of just how numb the shock has left us. The constant movement of early grief with the lists of things we are supposed to do to settle what remains of our loved one: the visitors, the food, the services, the financials, and contending with all their belongings. These tasks can distract us from processing our loss, and we can find ourselves in a freeze pattern of survival. We realize we are laying on the ground of our lives like a bird in shock after it flies into a window, stunned. All we can do is lie there and wait until our parts thaw and we come back online. This waiting looks completely different for each of us as our survival modes kick in.

For me it was a rollercoaster ride of furious action and tearful crashes. I could not, in my hypervigilant state, relax. I felt suspended, wings at the ready, to fly if needed – but never at rest. I could not stop. My mind raced to solve problems, it imagined problems and prepared, and it ruminated on past events. This was evidence of the plants that produced me, from birth to marriage, career, the births of our children and parenthood, and the current loss of my partner. The plants of my life each produced a single seed that grew with each new stage, containing memories and wisdom found deep within the DNA of this current seed – now planted in brand new soil. All I could do in the darkness was wait – wait, thaw, and feel.

Oh, This Bag is Heavy

Life, it beckons me to partake,
to dream a new dream.
But my baggage is heavy
I can't lift its weight.
Tempted to leave it
and move forward regardless,
but my baggage holds you.

I don't want to let you go –
though my mind has made itself numb,
the pain too great,
my system overwhelmed.
So, you stay in my bag
and I strap that baby on.
I start to walk toward the dream.

Oh, this bag is heavy
and the road unseen.
The distance great,
yet I dream a dream.

One step, then another,
I move slow some days,
faster on others.
I dare not look far down this path,
just in front,
where I am at present.
That's all I can muster.

Stopping at moments
when the rivers are deep.
Sometimes I climb stairs
that are nothing, but steep.
The rocks and the roots
reach out to grab me.

I stumble.
I fall.

My bag spills wide.
Its contents unwelcome
'cept you, my dear.
I sit for a moment
and cradle you near.
Then shake back my tears,
place you back in,
and walk on.

Oh, this bag is heavy
and the road unseen.
The distance great,
yet I dream a dream.

Our children surround me,
running circles,
unfettered.
They seem not to notice,
they seem not surprised,
at the pace I am keeping,
they come by my side.

Their hands slip in mine
as they look into my eyes,
searching for something –
something, I can't provide.

For I too am seeking,
I'm falling to pieces,
these little boys need hope
as my energy decreases.

But I can't let them down
so, I gather my strength.
I rise tall and I stand,
reaching down
I grab each by their hand.

Oh, this bag is heavy
and the road unseen.
The distance great,
yet I dream a dream.

I look down at my feet,
I see no ground at all.
Instead, I see flesh,
the hands of our friends
carry we three.

Through the dark and the deep,
the rivers and seas,
some old and some new,
some from long ago too,

come with desire
to help us journey on through.

Oh, this bag is heavy,
and the road unseen.
The distance great,
yet I dream a dream.

November 30, 2021

Rest A While

The birds and I,
we fly in agreement.
Gazing upon the speckled tapestry below.
The higher up we soar
the more sense it makes,
this picture unfolding.

But unlike my feathered friends,
these heights make me dizzy
and I pass out.
Plummeting.
Not yet ready for the view.
I awaken, before I meet the land,
shaking my head
I begin to regain composure.

The up currents against my slowly opening wings
sets me back on a course,
one I'm not yet comfortable with.
The tapestry too close,
I can't make out where I've come.
Flying blind.

I try to rise
but the winds have changed.
The downdrafts are strong now
and I fight for any distance between the ground and myself.
Weary,
I find a tree.

I sit resting among the naked branches –
fall has stolen the beauty
and winter cold has come,
hanging in the air.

I gaze about
trying to find somewhere to rest my weary eyes.
I find them welling with tears blinding me even further.
I decide to rest awhile
letting my searching take reprieve.

I sit with eyes closed
and I speak the mantra of the beloved:
soften,
rest awhile,
sit on this edge,
make space,
hold yourself in loving kindness.

Inhale.
Exhale.
Slowly now.
Sit.

With each breath
in,
I am weary
but will be made whole again.
Out,
I am letting go.

After some time
I open again,
lifting my face toward the sun.
The warmth fills me
as I breathe in.
I feel my strength returning.
The breeze on my face,
wings unfold
and the current lifts me without effort.

I'm hovering,
my favorite place to be.
Suspended,
weightless,
and for a moment,
peace is found.

December 5, 2021

Learning to rest in grief when the world around praises busyness and fast growth is one of the most courageous tasks for the griever. We learn to regulate our overwhelm by staying busy which merely masks and distracts from the ever-present pain. When the calm comes, we are often overtaken by the intensity of emotions and feelings we are not yet able to face. Exhaustion is a hallmark of staying busy and wearing facades, trying to appease a world so uncomfortable with our pain and suffering. Moments alone may bring a spiraling freefall of our story and it can be so disorienting.

Slowing down and finding our safe spaces to sit and rest becomes more and more imperative for our survival. Allowing emotions and feeling for a moment, closing our eyes and listening to the whispers of our soul expressing the sorrow deep inside, proves so much more fruitful than the constant distractions we frenetically seek refuge within. Slowing down and sitting with the scary and the painful may sound counter-intuitive, but it is part of the process of absorption. Coming to acceptance and nurturing ourselves in these spaces allows healing energy to flow. Growing around the huge losses stigmatized grievers face requires time to absorb the trauma we experienced. Our systems slowly start to come online as we process within safe spaces. Our souls can take a breath and say, "This thing happened, witness me in that moment. I was so scared. I felt so helpless." When we can allow ourselves to acknowledge the most painful truths, we can then hold space for those wounded parts of ourselves. While it requires work, it is also a form of rest from the watchful eyes of the world. We can fully be where we are as our seed germinates in the dark soil.

Widow's Lament

My soul is weary and worn.
The weight of it crushes my chest,
I can't breathe.

Loss after loss,
I long for a companion,
a lover,
a best friend –
someone to journey with.

I am not made to be alone.
I am not made for the loneliness of sorrow.
I want a hand to hold,
arms to enfold me.

Having been blessed once in this lifetime should be enough
but the losses make the emptiness that much greater.

They say I am strong.
They say I am powerful.

They don't sit in my body and experience this heaviness,
the extreme sorrow,
the ghostly memories.

They don't seem to see me.

They see a woman rising everyday
putting on her brave face
and moving.

They call that strength.

But I am not strong.
I'm beginning to implode.

I scream silent screams through the day,
shaking away memories and the tears that accompany.
I sit on my bed, in my car, in front of a screen, with friends
and the heaviness fills every fiber of me.

Places that were once full of love and life
are now drained and replaced by the hollowness of pain.
The hollowness is dark,
and the darkness heavy.

I try to hold on to hope,
resting in the kindness of friends
but it is not enough.

It is beautiful,
but not enough.

I've known the love of a man,
the love of one who accepted me in my most weak and
vulnerable places,
the love of a man who saw me as beautiful, including my faults,

who saw through the bravado and into my soul,
who held me in my fears,
wiped away tears,
journeyed through pain and loss,
supported me as I brought life into this world,
who trusted me and shared himself,
who allowed me to love him,
who changed and grew alongside me.

I've known what it feels like to let this beloved man down,
to not be enough,
to have all my attempts fail,
to not know how to help him heal,
to be so afraid, that I could not carry him,
to watch his strength fade and crumble away,
to watch him wrestle with distortions and fear,
to watch him pace in repetitive lies,
to watch the darkness engulf him and strangle the life out of him,
to watch him beg for death to take him
until he decided to take away his own beautiful life from us.

I cannot unsee what I've seen.
I cannot shake the ghostly memories that haunt me.
I cannot distract myself away from this.
He comes to me in dreams
and through apparitions,
memories,
and our children.

He comes to me through the hawk and the heron,
and here, only here,

is relief,
reprieve,
peace.

But those fade
and I am back in loneliness.

I am so over the lessons of life,
the relentlessness,
the constant ebb and flow,
they leave me weary,
my soul is tired.

The kindness and beauty of life exist
and they are lovely.
But their power is lost in the grief of the loss of them.

I am so weary my friends.
So.
Very.
Weary.

December 7, 2021

Held by a Sliver

Grief
Grieving
What was
Is no more
The dreams
The hopes
The comfort
The familiar
The joy
The peace
The frustrations
The fighting
The making up
The growth
The bettering of ourselves
The held hands
The soul tie
The connection
The perseverance
The life we created
The love
Falling in love watching you parent
Falling in love with how you love
It's all missing
It's all gone
And that sliver of a moon
Shining through the dark sky
Whispers to me
Calling to me to fix my eyes upon it

To let it hold me
To let it shine in the darkness of my soul
Wondering what in life will be my moon
Now that you are gone

January 20, 2022

Be With Nature

Watching the storm clouds,
sitting in the moment,
just being.

He was good at just being.

He could just sit and be.

While the rest of us were moving about,
playing,
imagining,
restless.

He could just be.

Be with his humanness.
Be with nature.
Be with himself.

I'm sure there was an ocean of thoughts and
daydreams on most occasions,
but
in nature, he could sit for hours.

I often wondered what was going through his mind
as he stood looking out over the vista,
but I was busy within myself.
We gave each other space
to be with our thoughts,
to be with our selves.

It was our way.

All while watching our little men be with themselves.

Together
but
with space.

Space to be.
To be human.

I miss my human.
Every.
Single.
Second.
His absence seems to have infected my ability to just be.
His presence gifted me the space of calm,
security,
comfort,
being.

The calming regulation of being loved and of loving another,
the sympatico,
the coming together,
being home for each other.

Learning to regulate on my own is a tricky path,
a path I am learning to navigate.
So grateful for my lovely tribe
as they carry me through this grief journey.

January 23, 2022

Through

You can't bypass grief,
you must go through it,
wade in it,
push your way through it,
hopefully not drown in it.
You must be in it
if you want to heal,
to grow,
to progress.
Feel it,
experience it,
be lonely in it,
make mistakes in it,
realize in it,
awaken in it,
weep in it,
laugh in it,
remember,
forget,
grasp where the old and the new collide,
create in it,
hold space in it,
collapse in it,
rest in it,
wrestle with it,
share it.
You must go through the journey of it,
find self-compassion in it,
forgiveness and hope.

You must hold on to hope,
feeling your lost one,
experiencing them,
missing them,
longing,
all while going through it all.

January 28, 2022

Past Dreams

Through the mountains we wandered,
dreaming up our later years.
Finding places that entranced us,
mesmerized us,
spoke to our hearts.
Places of beauty
barely touched
and when touched,
done so with care.
Seeing the old,
the abandoned,
enchanted.
Cathedral rocks
looming high above,
casting shadows on rivers.
Snowcapped mountain tops,
eagles,
hawks,
giant crows and ravens,
cawing –
announcing their arrival,
sweeping in front of us.

January 30, 2022

The past comes in and out of view so many times as we heal. A beautiful thing begins to happen the deeper we go, some of the scary and heartbreaking moments are slowly replaced by cherished moments. Where once I could only remember him as the ravaged man, sick from the medicine they gave him to help him; I began to have flashes of him making our boys laugh or creating opportunities to help us all experience the pleasures of life. Both good and bad memories arrive at their own will and speak to us, helping us process a life that was. Desperately trying to make sense of a story that existed but feels like someone else's reality; our mind regenerates thoughts, feelings and sensations. All the while, our system is crying out for us to move into what is our present reality and the two wrestle within us – the past and the present. A dramatic and soulful interplay starts a rebirth and our root shivers beneath the soil as it gains the strength to find a way to birth a sprout.

That Girl

That girl is no more
She only existed with him
He saw her
She saw him
They had a world all their own
Dreams
Inside jokes
Experiences
Understandings
Perseverance
Love
All
Their
Own
Redefining
Reinventing
All on hold
As grief grabs on
I miss that girl
I miss that boy

February 2, 2022

Bracelets

This is not what I pictured,
where I thought I'd be.
All new,
and not the good sort of new.
Collecting bracelets that tell stories,
stories of love lost,
of disease,
of supportive friendships.
Reminders of a story,
one not chosen
rather one thrust upon us.

With your loss
my body began to fail,
turning on itself,
attacking its life source.
Insult to horrifying injury.

Being part of an unwelcomed club,
the widowed and fatherless.
The club of those who forever grieve,
who lost the one who understood
and was understood,
who was the life force.

But the collection carries reminders
of friendship,
of support,
of courageous friends who come,

who carry,
who show up,
who remind of the beauty that still exists.

I wear them –
rotating them
adjusting them
seeing them daily.

They bring me to you, my love.

February 5, 2022

Shortly after his death, I found myself doubled over from pain that echoed the aching in my heart. I waited for days; it did not subside. I drove myself, alone, to the hospital – a moment he would have been there for had he been alive. The treatment I received was terrible, I was treated like an addict and largely ignored until one beautiful soul entered my room and saw me. She saw something was truly wrong and stepped in to care for me. I was diagnosed with an orphan disease, one that had begun to kill my left kidney, and was wreaking havoc on my vertebral and renal arteries, leaving me with damage that could kill me. I was hospitalized for over a week, and friends stepped in to care for me.

Many nights I could barely stand the pain in my head, I looked out my window at the mausoleum at the cemetery, a beacon mere yards from where the ashes of my love now rested. I felt both the comfort of him looking over me and the ironic twist of having to proceed in this life without him. I wept often, and while part of me resonated with the words he penned in his disease, I wanted to live, and I wanted to die. I wanted to join him. Yet my heart cried out for life, reminding me of our two beautiful boys, I knew I had to fight and live. I had to sit with the fear that I too could die, and these two dear souls we brought into this world could end up with no parents. I was so angry at how my story was playing out. It made no sense to me. I fought, I fought to accept this was my path, I fought to live for our babies, I fought to give them a different story than their father, I fought so I could realize the dreams I had to help other women. The fighting did not look noble, it was fought in my utter weakness, clad in a laced up blue gown and adorned with IV's and needles, bruises from blood draws and swollen limbs from all the fluids being pumped into my body. I fought with the support of beautiful friends who visited and lifted me up, encouraging me with love. I left ready to heal, to become stronger. I left ready to grow around my grief.

Say His Name

Say his name
Duncan
Daddy
My love
Honey

Say it
Speak it
Lest he be forgotten

Don't shy away
Share stories
Memories
Moments

He was here
He lived
He thrived
He gave
He cared
He hurt
He cried
He mourned
He grieved
He laughed
He did handstands
He camped
He loved
He fathered

He played
He was serious
He taught
He was home
He was safe
He was best friend
Friend
Son
Husband
Support
Intelligent
Thoughtful
Kind
Generous
He knew how to BE
Nature lover
Bird watcher
Provider

My love

He was here

Say his name
Duncan

February 25, 2022

The Universe

The universe feels so lonely without you in it.

Grief waves grow.
Every second,
new
more powerful waves arrive
washing over me.

As I look up to catch my breath
the vastness of the night sky
engulfs me,
swallows me whole,
capturing my attention
and then my smallness
wanders in.

And the universe feels suddenly so very lonely.

Captivated by the loneliness
my heart grows heavy in my chest.
I can't breathe I miss you so.
I don't understand the universe without you in it.

Your spirit must be somewhere?
Where did your energy,
your life force go?
Where are you now?
Are you up with the stars?
Are you down here with the hawk and the heron?

Did you fade into nothingness?

I hope the heavens are cradling you,
bringing peace to you.
That you are looking down
watching in wonder at how brave,
how strong,
how incredible
our boys are.

That you see me.
That you know how very loved you are,
And always were.

That the stars now light the way,
and truth surrounds you
as the bright moon feeds your soul.
That the secrets of the universe now sing their songs
and you understand what this is all about.

Oh, the dark night sky,
lit by constellations,
may it hold space for you,
for us.

Love always,
Heather

February 28, 2022

Stirrings

Flashbacks,
moments,
memories of how it started,
they flood me as we enter the season,
the time you got sick last year.
The excitement,
mixed with unrest,
a stirring.
Our spirits knew
but our mind could not conceive.
We did not know.
Well, maybe you did.
Maybe that's why you chose God?
Maybe that's why all the sleepless nights,
the purging and sorting,
the letting go of mementos.
They held more significance than they should have.
They held you, became your identity,
you got lost in the stories of them.
So many fears came too
and the nightly barrage of anxious thoughts
stole your sleep.
Mental and physical illness set in.
I misunderstood,
I thought if you got to the other side,
if you reached your goal,
if you pushed through your fears ...
If I had only known.
You didn't share

and when you did,
it made no sense.
Why didn't I see you,
the you, you needed me to see?
These memories,
these flashes of you,
they plague me,
break me.
They steal my breath.
They stop my heart,
then make it race.
My mind spins
out of control
and I'm bewildered
and intoxicated,
nauseous.
I fucking miss you!
I am so sorry I didn't see!
I didn't see YOU!
I felt so helpless.
I was letting go of all I knew too,
I was embracing this change,
for you,
for your dream.
I was overwhelmed with the longest to do list.
I was teaching our kids,
I was busy trying to find a place for us to settle,
to find areas with good schools
that were affordable,
I was organizing,
trying to keep everything and everyone afloat.

I embraced this change,
for you,
for me,
for our family.
But you kept trying to jump ship.
I kept trying to pull you back on
searching for ways to get you excited
for YOUR own dream job,
for the change YOU put into motion.
I got excited for it.

You did not.

You got lost.

We stopped too late.

These memories,
these flashes,
instill shame,
regret,
dismay,
disbelief.
They reignite helplessness,
fear.
They take me to you,
but not YOU –
the sick you,
the broken you,
the lost and terrified you,
the you that stopped seeing us,

the shell of my best friend, protector, lover, father to our children.
I am so broken now.
How am I supposed to stand and carry this?
How am I supposed to be strong for our babies?
How am I supposed to find the determination to carry on,
when
I fucking miss you so much?
This is so weighty,
so heavy,
so unbearable.

March 15, 2022

Masking

Put on that smile
Pretend a while
Move forward
And keep busy
Pack these big emotions up on the inside

Go to bed
Get up
All the while
Carrying this painful load
And it just never lets up

More than missing
This grief keeps insisting
Taking up space and time
Filling every corner of my mind
Til it leaks out
Spills out
Floods

Worse by the weeks
Aimlessly wandering
Trying hard to grab on to tools once learned
But it seems I've forgotten how to use them

Moments
Memories
Flashes
Bring me to my knees

And the weeping comes and goes
With a will all its own

My love
I can't feel you
I haven't in a long while
You've been missing before you actually left
And I miss my strong companion
I miss every part of you
Put on that smile
Pretend a while longer
Move forward
Stay busy
Examine these big emotions
And consider sharing them
Start to grow around the grief

March 26, 2022

Imagine

Some days
I like to imagine
coming around the corner
seeing him there,
on the couch,
snuggling a kiddo.

Then I feel a swell of emotion
and imagine running to him,
crawling in under his other arm
and snuggling in tight,
wrapping my arms around his back and soft belly,
kissing his face and crying.
Yes, crying.
Because I know it isn't real,
I can't do that.
But if I could,
I'd likely sit in his lap
and weep.
I'd press into his chest
and whisper "sorry."
Sorry that this happened to you.
Sorry that life played a cruel joke.
Sorry that you were stolen from us.

We love you!
We miss you with every breath we take.
Each inhale
and exhale.

Grief never ends,
it never leaves.
I'm told we have to grow around it
for it surely never gets smaller
because it's love
and love is eternal.

Others will move on
and we are left fragmented.
Having to learn how to be who we are now
without him,
to form a new identity
while grappling with memories,
dreams,
and hopes
we all created together.

Moment by moment,
step by step –
It's something like movement…

March 31, 2022

In the darkness of the soil, my root was growing down with each wave of grief processed and as I absorbed the fears invading my time of rest. My insides continued to expand as the processing deepened and though the coldness of others caused me to contract at times, the sun always returned and filled me with the energy needed to keep going. I discovered the importance of reading what I could absorb and connecting with other grievers who understood the doubts and fears I found surrounding me.

I relaxed into awe as my being expanded with each mental and emotional victory. With time, I began to see myself awakening and it gave me hope. I was slowly gaining confidence in my ability to survive this loss.

Reflecting

Sitting in a coffee shop
trying not to cry
as I find myself completing tasks to deepen my knowledge.
Surrounded by men,
some attractive,
others not so much.
I find myself wondering if you are my one and only
and this hurts my heart,
because I miss you so very much.
I overhear someone sharing their experience at the Broadmoor,
a place where you took me the last anniversary you were healthy.
Tears swell.
I find it difficult to be without you.
I miss you so very much.
I am acutely aware NO ONE can ever fill your shoes.
You and I grew up together,
we lived together.
You were my heart,
my home,
my ONLY safe human.
You, my love, could calm me,
could regulate me,
could hold me safe.
You and only you knew all of me
and stood by my side,
regardless of my moods and crazy moments.
How could I even consider another?
No one grew up with me, as you did.
No one understood me.

How could they?
You were there when things with my father unfolded.
You were there when my sister's marriage fell apart.
You walked with me through miscarriages and pregnancies.
Babies.
Deaths.
I was there with you too.
Your dad,
Your dad … what a shitty impact.
I try not to blame him.
I try not to hold him accountable for your illness.
Genetics are cruel sometimes
and now, we passed those on to our boys.
Damn!
How do I safeguard them?
How do I protect our babies?
How?
How is it possible to provide them the tools to withstand what
may come?
What will fall upon them?
I am so scared they too will battle this disease.
Damn, babe, I miss you so much.
I really want your hand to hold.
I fear I was not enough for you.
That in my own depression.
I didn't see yours.
Why didn't I ask instead of just taking mental notes?
Why did I believe you were so strong?
You were so good at putting on that brave face.

April 4, 2022

Flashbacks

I took the kids to school today
and as I watched them walk up the stairs, I spoke to you.
"Our boys are going to school today."
Though I initially said this to the sweet dog beside me
I repeated it in my mind to you.
Then the flood gates were set free
and I wept the entire drive home.
Flashbacks to how much agony you were in,
how you were mentally and physically tormented.
All I could think, is that if I had known
I would have made you sit in my arms,
I would have held you.
I was so afraid.
I felt so helpless.
I had no idea what was happening to you.
It has been suggested by a therapist that you likely were struggling
with a bipolar episode.
That makes sense since your father and likely your grandfather
struggled too.
To set in so late in life
is a thing I didn't know possible.
The meds clearly made you worse
but you were already struggling before.
Oh, my love, I miss you so incredibly.
I don't know how to do this without you.
I don't really want to do this without you.
The boys need their dad and I, frankly, really need you.
Some days I just go through the motions,
others, all I can do is sit and stare.

And days like today, the emptiness feels so great
all I do is weep openly.
It is not right that you had to go like that,
you deserved so much better.
You were the kindest man I have ever known.
I know that I will never find anyone like you.
You were my person.
You were my life partner.
I am so very lonely without you.

April 6, 2022

Juxtapose

Spring
Energizing
Rebirth

And also

Visceral
Beginning of the end
A quick spiral

A favorite
And
A painful reminder

Life always presents
Juxtapositions

This
And
That

Both can exist
And do

April 26, 2022

One of the great moments of awakening for me as a griever was the day I learned to replace the word, but, with the word "and". And opened possibilities within my grief. And gave me permission to both grieve and live life. And came to me as the rains came to encourage the seed, reminding it of its purpose. The rains came and the soil expanded, enclosing the seed in an embrace of encouragement. And offered me the belief that I could walk forward with my grief, showing me it was a gift just as much as it felt like a giant burden. Opposites can exist and juxtapositions are found so often within grief.

Where Are You

When you left your body
did your mind return to you?
Did your love and wisdom,
your great big heart,
Did it find its way back to you?
Did your spirit leave and go away?
Did it stay?
Does it in fact come on the wings of the birds?
Do you ride the winds,
and dance in the grass?
Do you watch over us?
Do you feel free?
Do you weep when you see our boys?
Do you see our pain,
our broken hearts?
Where is your beautiful energy now?

April 29, 2022

Oh, Grief

Grief,
a monstrous beast
and also
a brilliant internal processing
of that which we cannot comprehend.
It leaves you on your knees one moment
and laughing at some absurdly dark humor the next.
It floods you with glorious memories
then takes you out with a scent.

It brings insecurities,
fears,
and reactivity.
while also birthing
compassion,
depth,
and purpose.

It changes you.
Every.
Single.
Part of you.

Navigating this shit without you is ironic
for you are the one person who could have helped me navigate it
with any ease.

Love is alive
and my love for you lives on.

So angry that you were stolen away from us.

May 2, 2022

Be Present

Savor every moment.
Make peace with the challenges of the moment.
Breathe.
Close your eyes and just listen,
listen to the sounds of your loved ones:
their laughter,
their chatter,
their sniffles,
and sneezes,
their bickering and fighting.
Listen to what they are truly saying
not just their words or actions.
Seek their hearts.
Are they silently crying out
for validation,
comfort,
control?
It's easy to miss amid daily chaos.
Are they pouring out love in the only ways they know how?
Do you notice it as such?
Sit down and take that extra moment.
Really listen.
There is always time to pause,
if even just for a second.
So much is asked of us
and we often feel we don't have an extra second.

But the irony is
that second may just make the load we carry
a little bit lighter.

July 15, 2022

There are moments in our grief, where we draw upon our good memories to soothe ourselves. Where we look for what we loved to quiet the pain of what happened. This helps us build our capacity towards resilience, as it fosters within us joy and gratitude for having known our person. For the seed, this is part of its DNA, it is the part that makes a plant resilient to certain forces of nature, telling it to expand or contract. When the memories are positive, expansion can occur in grief because it is in these moments where the gratitude urges us to want to choose life.

Remembering You

The gentleness of your smile,
the comfort of your embrace,
the genuine nature of your being,
the way you knew –
You just knew,
the way you gave and received,
the silliness,
the truthfulness,
and passion,
the way you taught,
the way you learned,
the way you worked on yourself
and allowed for others to do the same,
the way you pushed yourself,
acknowledged yourself,
knew yourself,
the way you were fearless,
a fighter,
a truth seeker,
the way you made others feel,
the way your smile lit up everything,
the way you entertained,
and the way you stepped into the shadows,
the absolute joy you expressed for our boys,
the way you did life
when you were you,
always 100%,
a perfect 10.5.
I miss you so incredibly!

August 20, 2022

Moving on with You

I was who I was, because of you.
It was your strength that held me up
when things got rough.
You carried me
when I had no strength.
You were there for me
to squeeze at the birth of our boys.
When I was scared
your chest a constant safe resting place.
In your arms
I felt comfort and protection and love.
The absence of you
has left me feeling vulnerable,
lonely,
and isolated.
I am surrounded with beautiful friends
but compared to you,
everything else fails.
You were my strength,
my rock,
my very best friend.
I don't know how to do this life without you.
The hole you've left seems to grow by the day.
As the year has passed
and rounding into another,
I find myself longing for you.
As the seasons change
I am forced to move on.
But moving on does not mean without you,

you are forever in my thoughts,
in every cell of my being,
and in every breath.
Late at night I long for you,
there is no peace without you by my side.
I am strong,
it is true –
but my strength is not my own
and now that you are gone
my strength feels like it is fading.
Our boys miss you.
I miss you.
We miss your light.
We miss your joy.
We miss your adventurous spirit.
Through the day
I cry as I long for you,
for your hand to reach for mine.

October 20, 2022

Memories: Call to Action

I thought you'd be by my side
until the day I died.
That you'd hold my hand as I breathed my last breath
just as you held it every time I reached for you.
I thought we'd go journey
like gypsies
along the coast
taking in all the beauty of creation.
That our home would be wherever we chose to be
in any given moment.
I thought we'd have time to figure out a way to make it all come
true.
That the safety I had in you was a sure thing,
a forever thing
because you were strong.
You knew how to protect –
always thinking,
always planning,
always aware,
never trusting the world to have our back.
Too wise.
too knowledgeable,
deeply aware of the big picture
you did not trust blindly.
Yet you faced the world with compassion,
empathy.
Unless of course they bristled your feathers,
then you'd listen,
ready to speak up,

to fight and defend.
You were a defender
and the world is lesser for the loss of you.
I am too.
Your presence freed me to let my guard down.
You were my trusted home.
You were the only soul who ever saw me completely.
I am so lonely for you!
You,
my greatest teacher,
taught me to love
and that I am worthy to be loved.
Trying to find where to place the love that was reserved only for
you.
Not married,
not single,
yet both,
and neither.
Damn, my love,
the quandary of my remaining days
however long they be...
Friends,
do not take the days with your love for granted.
Don't let the stupid shit separate you.
Let go of the stuff that's petty, annoying, and dull.
Rest in the boredom of long relationships.
Breathe in the mundane.
For surely, if you love, you will experience loss someday,
it's just a given of life.
Kiss,
embrace,

dance,
give those knowing glances,
speak the language only known between you,
let your history speak
your privileged knowledge.
Cradle and never forget gratitude.
If you know love
you have been given a gift.
See it.
See them.
Listen.
Quiet the inner critic.
Sooth the needy child inside
so you can be present,
so you can love and be loved.

October 22, 2022

Just BE

"We too are nature."
What if we lived our lives without the striving to do better?
We say we want to "be" kinder, "be" faster, "be" wiser, "be"
calmer..."be" this or that.
But that is all DOing, not Being
We strive to BEcome perfection
when perhaps
as nature
we already are.
What if we are exactly where we need to BE?
Growing,
changing with the tides of the seasons we are in,
sometimes active and thriving,
others barren and dormant.
One not better than the other,
equally important.
What if
in the barren season we just rest
instead of longing to do or BEcome more?
Oh, I've fallen for the trappings of society
telling me how I should "be,"
when really
it's telling me what I should DO.
Never settled.
Never calm.
Never allowing what is
to simply BE.
Nature doesn't push itself to be more than what it was meant to be.
It is beautiful for it.

What am I meant to be?
Can I stop striving to find out
and instead, just be it?
Allowing the pain to shape me
without resistance?
Just growing as the now crooked tree once did,
impacted by its environment
yet remaining a tree.
It shows its weathering.
It is more interesting and beautiful for it.
Surely it did not think,
"I am ruined from this drought! Or this storm, or this person
carving into me!"
It simply kept reaching for the sun,
living its cycles.
We are nature.
We are Beings.
I hope one day
I allow myself the freedom to just be...

October 31, 2022

Charms Around My Neck

Before,
the necklace carried only the charms of our lovely boys,
a bird, to remember the babies who didn't join us,
and a stone to remember my beloved granny.
It's heavier now
our wedding bands in tow,
always close to my heart.
Always a reminder of the greatest loves in my life.
Love is eternal.
And though this earthly plain no longer holds you,
you are forever written into my story.
A story I will tell to all who are kind enough,
brave enough
to listen.

Humanity lives on in the stories,
past and present,
honestly portrayed,
bravely sharing the truths encountered by all.

Your story will live on.
The beautiful,
the brave,
the courageous truths of you,
walking in the DNA of our babies,
woven into the stories they remember.

Forever in my heart.

January 27, 2023

Ponderings

Early mornings
I rise
From dreams with you
And so many without you
And when I wake
My hand still reaches for yours
It still searches
Alongside my longing heart
For any piece of you
Any trace
Any brief passing of your spirit
My mind races
Rushing
Searching
And it catches
Along with my breath
Fleeting images
Memories
Shadows
Nothing
The eerie darkness
Filling with dread
As the feeling of your last days arise
My mind just can't
Try as it does to fathom what took you
What stole your beautiful light

February 7, 2023

Suicide is not easy to contend with when you've lost your beloved, your father, or your son. Wrapping your head around their life, the process that stole them can be extremely daunting. Knowing there were things they kept inside, didn't share, and carried on their own is excruciating. Being well-read enough to know not to let the inner critic point fingers, accuse, and blame is not always enough. Sitting gently with oneself is no small task. It's a continual winding river of rapids with few calm spots. Because of the fierceness of the rapids, growth is slow, because survival is often the focus. Choosing the direction to take often depends on the waves that come. Here is a true test of the coveted resiliency society holds on a high pedestal.

To the outsider, we may appear to be doing well. We are moving forward, going about the business of life. Our lives seem to blend into the culture around us. Inside however, we carry the weight of our loss. Outside, we laugh often, running about and carrying on. Yet the grief sneaks out of the cracks found in our broken vessels, and it's seen, spotted, noticed. We may be surprised at who will scoop it up as it spills out and hold it with us as they walk alongside. Some know what to do with it, while others are lost on how to carry it. That's okay. We are all figuring this out.

This cracked vessel continues to figure out what to fill the cracks with...putty? Gold? The light from the outside? Still testing my options. Or maybe, as the coat of the seed bursts open as it grows, we don't fill the cracks of our vessel and allow ourselves to simply become what we are becoming.

Listen, She Will Speak

To heal,
you must connect with your body.
You must release what your body remembers.
You cannot do that in distraction,
you do it through tears,
retelling of stories,
placing your hands on your heart and breathing.
Breathing deeply
into the spaces
that tighten,
constrict,
and
choke hold your heart –
making captive your being
as you shelter yourself from the hot glow of sorrow.
Into the wild you run
as the building tension tightens
and you move your body
to release.
to let loose,
to freedom
from the pain of grief,
the stories etched into immune systems,
emotional responses,
and brought forth by the triggers of daily existence.
The body screams to be seen,
held,
acknowledged,
set free.

In sickness it cries.
In mental chatter it begs.
It will be seen.
Run to it.
Embrace it.
Hold it as a child in need of comfort.
This is what grief demands of us.
This is what your healing demands of you.
Courage dear soul,
be brave,
listen to your body,
your mind.
It is speaking!
Curiously ask what it needs
and then,
be still,
listen.
Compassionately
create safety
and she will speak.
She wants you to heal.

February 26, 2023

Wise Warrior

Grief
She is steadfast
Unyielding
Ever present
She reminds
She reveals
She puts on full display
All that was
all that wasn't
All that could have been
Inescapable

Grief
Tugs
Pulls
Rips apart
And then the carnage reveals
The deepest needs
Desires
Longings
The places of greatest need
The deepest of wounds
Yearning

Grief
A healer
A sage
A warrior of wisdom
Will sit with you

Cradle you
Put back the pieces
Showing each along the way
Telling the true stories
Dispelling your myths
Rebuilding

March 5, 2023

I've witnessed the wisdom of grief, the power to transform. I'm not sure how long this rebuilding will take or what processes grief still has for me. I'm certain she has many more processes to unveil, and I'm certain courage will be needed. How I've mustered the strength to come to this place is a mystery. Journeying without him by my side is no small feat. I hate it often. My tears, ever present, show up more frequently than I imagined they would. Everywhere I go, reminders of our 21-year journey. Sometimes, I want to run. I want to go somewhere far from here. But I stay, to feel him in any way I possibly can. To find his energy wherever it still resides. He is in our babies, the mountain roads, in the sunlight dancing on the aspen leaves, in the hawks still flying overhead, in the shows we once watched, in the bed bought for a once aching back, in the photos, the conversations with friends, in the cars bought thoughtfully to keep us safe or more economical, in the dresser drawer still reserved for him, in the rings around my neck and resting on my finger, in my cells and in my heart, forever and always. He was mine. He is mine. He was one of a kind, and I was so fortunate to have been his. I walk with Grief, for She knows him too. She is our love.

On The Edge

Searching for joy in grief
is like playing on the edge of a frozen, snow-covered lake.
It's beautiful,
you want to explore it,
but you must be cautious.
You see the tracks of those before you,
brave individuals that tested the integrity of the icy surface.
But you don't trust it.
So, you stay on the shoreline,
you play within the safety zone.
You listen to that voice inside telling you to go no further.
You remain on the shoreline
flitting about.
But there remains this inner tug,
this desire to step out bravely.
Your inner alarm system simply won't allow it
so, you play on the edge
holding both desire and fear.

March 18, 2023

One must feel safe to experience pure, unadulterated joy. Grievers often long for the joy felt before the sting of loss colored everything they do. I'm finding that in profound loss, many of us lose a sense of safety. This world now holds a threat that everything we hold dear can be taken. It was always there before, but we could idealistically overlook it. We had the freedom to buy into the words of our positivity culture. We had the childlike ability to live for what made us feel good. Carefree. But, with the entrance of deep loss, the world begins to feel more threatening. Fear steps in. Emptiness creates a vacuum where once stood a beautiful life-giving soul.

There are many things we are taught to do throughout life along with accolades received for doing them "right." The intense pressure to be resilient and to pick ourselves up by our bootstraps essentially bypasses our pain as we try to keep those around us comfortable. No one wants to be reminded of the potential reality of their deepest fear. We are asked to put on a smile and get out there and live. Learning what it means to not bypass or get stuck is crucial for us to grow our roots down into the soil and to begin to grow a shoot toward the heat of the sun.

Within Reason's Arms

The Trees I climb now
are tall and wide,
with branches low
but often too high,
beyond my reach.
I've found them in the valley.
We walked through the valley of the shadow of death
and we feared the evil that came –
taunting,
teasing,
messing with us in the darkness of night.
For You fell silent to our cries,
You turned your head, like the Judas who denied you.
You handed us over.
No rod
nor staff to comfort.
Broken promises to the fervent hearts who finally heard your call
and sought your face.

This is life,
I reason with my weary soul.
There was no promise of ease,
only words in a book
now dusty and abandoned,
with tear-stained pages
and forgotten notes scribbled in the margins,
and a faith tainted by experience.
A book who's words
inscribed on a broken heart

feel hollow.
Within the casing of misunderstood meaning,
interpreted by fallible men
who proposed the words for their own endeavors.

Turning from the knowledge of my youth
toward the truths unfolding within broken places,
seeing life through new lenses,
through the fabrics of grief –
the clouds that cover weeping eyes,
and letting the old hymns dance upon the edges of my dreams.
While skepticism fades into the energy that charges all of life
the gods of old laugh into the shadows
and reason trips around
stumbling boldly
in plain view,
mocking interpretations made in earlier years.
Spinning behind me
it reaches around,
it's hands forming new spectacles with which I can now see things
once undisclosed.
Its arms weigh on my shoulders
and its laughter rings through my ears.
At my feet,
old glasses pile up.
Broken.
Smashed.
Destroyed.
Turning within Reason's arms,
I face it now
curiously searching its depths.

Nothing exists there
and it vanishes.
Weight lifting from my shoulders
I float upward,
watching the glasses disappear,
the atmosphere fade.
Surrounded by nothing and yet the light of everything.
Neither dark
nor light,
just existence.
Fading into it
I disappear.

April 6, 2023

Living On

Can't sleep,
I miss you too much.
I was grumpy all day
and realize this season is the season we began to lose you.
Grief does not end my friends,
it just doesn't.
There are no stages,
no magic one year mark.
His loss is not a lesson for me or my boys.
I do not have to look for beauty in it.
I know it's difficult to witness my grief.
I know it hurts to see my struggle.
I know.
But as deep as my love for him
so is my grief.
And time reveals just how deep our love is (It's still there!).
I know I've changed,
am changing.
I don't reach out in the same ways.
My previous struggles have morphed.
In some ways I've become more open,
in others, more protective.
I am still vulnerable and share too much,
but it feels different.
I am more convinced that we are all energy,
our bodies are simply our earth suits.
Perhaps when we die, our energy moves on.

My beloved is somewhere.
Some of his energy lives on in our boys,
the rest perhaps has joined the chorus of other departed souls
singing the songs of the universe.

April 17, 2023

Another Anniversary

23 years ago
you took my hand.
I was scared of life
and you opened me up.
I knew, with you by my side
I could figure it out.
You were constant and strong,
beautiful and kind,
interesting,
brave,
funny,
wise.
You were the one for me.
You just knew,
you knew.
You knew what it took to calm my anxious heart.
With you, I felt safe,
at home.
And though the years were sometimes difficult,
and we were so very human,
we fought our way through.
You were worth fighting for.
You were worthy of my love.
You were my world.
I love You forever and always.

On this morning,
I don't want to get out of bed.
I don't want to face a world without you.

I don't want to.
But we created two of the most beautiful little men
who need me to want to.
I am working on it,
I am.
I continue to rise
though exhausted by the nights of longing for you.
I continue to move through my days
smiling,
laughing,
giving,
learning,
and growing.

I forge ahead
to keep you alive,
to honor you.

Though sometimes it still feels like I'm surviving,
I'll keep moving,
I'll keep looking for brighter days.

The last tender words you spoke,
"You're my angel,"
echo in my mind.
Baby, you were my angel too.

May 13, 2023

Then and Now

Days away from two years without you.
I can't even express the emotions experienced right now.
We are continuing forward.
We keep on keeping on.
The past is behind,
yet ever present.

My longing for you
grows.
My love for you
increases.

Losing you as we did
left permanent scars,
flash backs,
unwanted memories.
Revisiting places we went in your illness,
an effort to create new memories,
searching for silver linings.

Letting go of the past,
an enduring task.
I won't be shackled.
I won't be held prisoner.
I will keep on moving toward light.
I will express.
I will grow.
I will share.
I will keep an open heart.

But damn,
it doesn't stop the missing.

Love you forever and always,
then and now.

June 2, 2023

Birthing the Warrior Spirit

I am strong enough.
I have born witness to my capacity to keep going
even when I am falling apart inside.
Daily I choose to keep moving,
to keep searching for joy,
to get up and out of bed
when my heart is keeping me there.
That is strength.
I will no longer balk
when people tell me I am strong.
Surviving is strength.
I accept that even though I don't have to be strong,
I am a WARRIOR.

June 15, 2023

Growth in grief, it's slow and sometimes requires deliberately changing your reactions into thoughtful responses. Early in grief I would have cringed if you told me how strong I am. Many grievers will shut you down for this compliment of awe. There are many reasons for this. For some, they feel so broken by their pain they can't fathom what the hell you are talking about. For others, the idea of being seen as strong is infuriating because they are angry that they have to be "strong." And still others will retort with, I'm not strong, I'm surviving. There is a distinction there, let's be clear about that and in early grief I argued this point often.

However, with the passing of time, I began to see that tenacity is needed to survive. It requires strength to get out of bed and face a world without our person. It requires strength to carry the weight of the loss every second of the day. It requires strength to put on a smile and search for joy because sometimes, it feels impossible. It requires strength to look outside your own pain and lift your kids up. It requires strength to allow your vulnerable parts to show. It requires strength to choose to move forward without the one person who helped you carry the weight of the world. Strength is required for survival. Yet in survival, we rarely feel strong, because we are still defining it from a previous lens.

I have learned to stop balking with anger because I didn't choose this path. Rather, I am gaining acceptance for the fact that this path chose me, and I am doing it. I am capable. I am surviving. Strength does not require I like it to exist. It simply shows up. It is not the enemy; it is our helper. I now take my strength by the hand, close my eyes, inhale deeply, and exhale in acceptance, trusting its guidance.

Exhausted Warrior

I awake in a wave,
This wave crashes,
showing the build-up of strong happy moments.
The wave is giant
and now, it's crashing down.

In dreams, my mind is hard at work within this wave,
and waking, I feel it crashing down.

Grief is unrelenting.
I'm weary.

An exhausted, wounded warrior.

My dream said it all.

It ended with me boxing,
wailing on the bag.
Then,
after one final round of intense punching and a final kick,
I collapsed,
crumbling to the floor weeping.

My inner being is doing what my ailing body can't,
discharging my physical grief.

Grateful for strong moments,
while struggling with the aftermath.

This is grief.

Still a warrior,
but an exhausted one.

June 16, 2023

Letting Go

The act of letting go –
it plays on repeat over and over again throughout life.
I close my eyes,
inhale,
and sit with this letting go.
What does it mean?
Having, grasping, owning, knowing.

Pause,
sit with it.

Now, exhale,
let it go.
Release it, free it, let it be.
Like breath,
Letting go is a constant part of life.

Breathing is effortless,
instinctual.

I suppose letting go can become like breathing
with practice,
with the knowledge that life is impermanent.

However,
unlike breath,
there are some things we hold on to –
we need to hold on to.

July 13, 2023

Survival IS Strength

Yes, I am strong.
Survival IS strength.
AND I am also exhausted.
Survival often involves fear,
putting out fires,
heavy lifting.
Managing my own emotions
and helping my kids with theirs.
Endless searching for ways to keep us alive
and thriving.
It means sitting with and facing my grief
while helping them with theirs.
It also means down days,
lying in bed,
binging shows,
crying into pillows,
yelling at God,
conversations with my love,
sleeping,
eating comfort food.
Some days,
I just want to be carried,
to not have to be strong.
This is why being called strong stings sometimes.
I'd rather have my partner here
helping me carry the load of life
and the grief left in his absence.
Survival is strength,

just not the strength of thriving.
There is a very real difference.

September 16, 2023

Somedays, no matter how far along you are in the grief "germination" process, there come times when you are just so weary, so exhausted, and it is incredibly difficult to rise up, to draw upon your resources. We can easily find ourselves returning to this place again and again. What do I know? How do I move forward? I don't feel like moving forward, I want to just sit today out and draw back inside and close my eyes as I listen to the wisdom of my soul, letting it guide me back to a place of growth and further expansion. Plants also rest to regain energy to continue growing, and so, we return again and again to our reserves, supporting ourselves.

As established, surviving is strength, yet here is another very important distinction – surviving is not the same as thriving. We may have the strength to continue moving through the day in and the day out, however, much like the seed as it sits in the dark soil, we must move from the darkness and reach toward the light if we are to become and live as we were made to live.

Not all plants grow at the same speed and thriving may take years for the seedling to truly establish itself. Our individual process will require us to look within and listen. I mean truly listen. What does your beautiful and unique soul need? What specific type of seed are you and how do you need to find nourishment and nurturing? Your specific timetable is beautiful, because it accounts for all that fills your coat, all the memories and experiences. Those require very distinct parts to heal and grow. Wounded and scared parts will require more time. We must learn to be gentle with our process, wrapping ourselves in self-compassion and love.

Weary

I'm trying.
I'm trying to do the things I love
but lately, it is just really hard.
I am exhausted.

As women, we carry so much.
As moms, even more.
As a griever,
so much.

I have been waking up in the wee hours from nightmares,
tossing and turning,
trying to nurture my own heart,
hold my own hand,
sit with my feelings.

In truth, I'm tired of feeling the feelings.

I know it's what we are supposed to do on our healing journey,
but I'm over it.

Also, I'm tired of carrying them alone.

I'm an open book.
But, lately, I just don't feel people really want to hear anymore.
I can't tell if that's true
or if I'm just sensitive to being a burden,
Or if I'm just so tired I don't have the energy to reach out.

This is a rough patch.

This is the grief journey.

Making beautiful things on the outside, while inside, there is a struggle going on.

Miss you every second of every day my love. We could sure use a boost.

October 13, 2023

Keep Going

I can't, and yet, I am.
Some days, grief is like this.
Nothing inside you wants to
and yet you do,
you keep going.

It must be part of the human spirit,
that thing that propels us
when everything feels hollow and scary.
It keeps us going.

I'm glad it's there.
I'm grateful.
I trust in a future where things will be different,
where I will have the energy once again
to actively seek joy.

I also know there are seasons
where the leaves die and fall away
and trees must rest,
naked and cold.

This is when they store up energy.

It's necessary.

We, too, must rest in barren times.

I try not to place expectations during these seasons.
Rather, let what comes in be what it is,
no judgement,
no "should,"
just raw emotion and thought.
And I hold them,
sit with them.
I'm learning to do this.
Loving kindness toward my hurt parts,
the parts that suffer.

I breathe in.
I breathe out.
Hands resting over my heart,
comforting
as I remind myself
all parts are welcome here.
Its vital work.

When my judge tries to resist
in the discomfort of new ways,
I hold it, too.
I see you.
You are scared.
You want to protect,
but we are safe.
In this moment,
we are safe.

We can get up
AND
we can rest.

Both are good.

November 2, 2023

It Takes Time

Once upon a time
we worked on regulating our nervous systems –
He, in nature,
myself, pairing mindful meditation and nature.

Then, he died.

My nervous system could not tolerate mindfulness anymore.

I let go of the practices I had started.

They are difficult to choose now.
I equate them with a time in my life that was so unbearable;
and what was meant to heal
has become a painful reminder.

I wonder if other grievers have experienced this?

I do not judge this aspect of my grieving process,
rather, I'm curious about it.

I have learned not to rush the process of grief,
it runs a course of its own.
Which in a society whose message is to be in control of your
reactions,
this "allowing" feels like inaction.
It's difficult because it feels like I'm allowing grief to run the show,
and that sounds ludicrous.

However, when I attempted to be in control
life rushed in,
reminding me this is not how it works.
Healing must happen first.
We can't bypass the stuff of grief.
It has a sneaky way of popping back up,
it shows up in our reactions –
despite our greatest efforts.
This is frustrating and can often leave us feeling defeated.

I found a natural return to a mindfulness technique I learned
from Tara Brach – RAIN
Recognize
Allow
Investigate
Nurture
Here is where the beauty of past practices arises,
parts of those former practices become embedded and become
our default in times of need.

We cannot control life
despite what we are told.
We can't always naturally control our reactions to it.
This is not a failing, but often a conditioned response to stimuli.
I do believe we can, however,
learn practices that will help us to take back the reins of our
reactivity.
That begins with recognition.
Here is where self-compassion and grace enter our stories.

Removing the judgement of the "shoulds,"
which tell us we should control our reaction,
frees us up to investigate the root cause of that reaction.
We can turn our attention to healing the root cause,
recognizing that I have an emotion,
allowing it to exist,
sitting with it in curiosity,
and nurturing what arises,
this is where healing begins.

Be kind to yourself.
It takes time.

November 7, 2023

Preparing to grow upward, when the time comes, requires incredible bravery. It is in this season when we accept the conditions in which we have been placed and as we learn to navigate the detractors that undoubtedly will come our way. It is important to remember these detractors, found within us, are here to keep us safe. They are the old defenses, the guards showing up as fear and anxiety, they hold the memories and make decisions based on previous experiences. These parts remember what brought us pain and suffering and show up in whatever form they decide we need. Sometimes anger, sometimes laughter, we must learn to navigate and grow around whatever shows up. It is in learning to befriend these parts where we can gain that acceptance.

Listening to the parts and sitting with them in self-compassion and loving kindness builds the resilience we once looked upon with frustration and distain. We begin to see glimpses of hope. Hope comes in as a powerful protector, reminding us of our potential. As we learn to listen, we also begin to get curious about why these emotions and feelings come as they do and when they do. When hope is met with fear or even distrust, we can ask why and begin to recognize patterns. These patterns show us areas to proceed cautiously into, and we gain strength with each attempt to move into the struggle. The struggle and resistance are where our roots gain strength.

It is in this season of grief where I remember telling those around me, "You know what? We are warriors! Think of all the things we carry on top of the normal day to day struggles." It was in this season where I began to honor the hard work I had been doing, and I wanted so desperately to share this with my fellow grievers. I wanted others to gain the strength to keep moving forward as I had, by acknowledging how incredibly hard they have been working.

This strength and knowledge do not mean we suddenly are healed, and grief no longer has a grip on us, in fact, quite the opposite is true. Because as we begin to change, new obstacles and reactive parts emerge. The thing is, we now have this little slice of hope to hold onto, and our outlook changes. Growing continues to be a struggle, and it is also something we begin to step more confidently into because we are beginning to trust our process.

SECTION FOUR

THE ENVIRONMENT: ORIENTATION AND LIGHT

Story of a Seed: Part Four

The other voices tried to speak up, but the sun's allure was far greater, and the seed simply said to the chorus of detractors, "I see you. I know you want to keep me safe. But this is what we are meant to do! We can do this! I know we can!" The voices fell to the background watching in amazement as our dear seed exploded open and reached a tiny, and very strong seedling to the surface.

"Ah! There you are!" cried the sun in delight, excited to see its friend. "You are so beautiful! Look at that brilliant shade of green you are! Simply amazing! I knew you had it in you!" The light of the sun filled the seedling with such energy it could not stop growing and reaching for its warm friend.

The seedling was in such awe at the sight of the outside world. It had forgotten what the blue sky looked like, how its old friend the wind felt, the beautiful songs of the birds, and all the colors! The seed had forgotten how many brilliant colors were above the surface of the soil. The seedling could only breathe out a wispy, "Oh my!" In a meditative stance, the seedling turned its leaves up toward the sun and its stem sent messages deep into its core, "We made it! This is why we exist! We are changing!"

The sun, the seedling, the world around, all paused for a glorious moment in absolute union. The connection they all felt was undeniable and so incredibly beautiful. They belonged to each other. They were all part of something. The energy of the sun brought life, the wind carried things to their destinations and strengthened them through creating resistance, the creatures feasted and kept balance, the soil held and nurtured life, and the rains brought expansion and quenched those who were parched and withering away. All things sustained each other. And the seedling – the seedling was beginning to see it fit into this beautiful cycle. Though it was still figuring out its exact purpose, it began to wonder if existing and growing were purpose enough.

The sun, having seen so many seedlings emerge could sense the new thoughts developing inside the seedling, "Don't get ahead of yourself dear one! Enjoy this moment, this exact moment right now. Bask in my warmth, let my light fill you with energy and enjoy the process of changing molecules within you. Let your cells exhale oxygen as you feel the wind moving you. Allow the moisture and the nutrients deep in the soil to sustain you in this moment. Rest a moment in the peace that comes with breaking through. You have earned it!" The sun's words felt like a warm caress, much like the mother plant as it cradled the developing seed.

Taking the words to heart, the seedling rested. Its old friend the wind came and gently rocked the seedling, stirring memories of the mother plant, holding it and rocking it as it grew. The seedling felt a longing for its mother and a strange sort of peaceful sorrow swept over the seed as it remembered. The birds sensed the sorrow and sang lullabies to the seedling, and the seedling rested in the energetic arms surrounding it.

Another powerful surge was felt deep within the ground, as the seed coat broke open fully and sent the seedling the loving energy placed deep within from the mother plant. "I am always with you! You carry me in your DNA, in your soul. As you remember me, remember how much I loved you. Let this love fill you and grow you. I still love you; your very life is a testament of this. I may no longer be with you in the way you once knew but look around you, I am there. When you are most quiet, you will feel my spirit flowing through all that lives."

The seedling inhaled the air around it and gently and slowly exhaled pure oxygen. "Thank you!" came a choir of a thousand voices. The seedling realized the sentient beings surrounding it were receiving its oxygen, it was giving them life. It was part of this cycle, just like the other seedlings and more mature plants that surrounded the seedling.

They all sat cradled together as the newness of spring awoke them all. This moment lasted for a long while and the wind awakened a dance within the seedling. Swaying to the rhythms of the energy and the songs of the birds and the croaking of the frogs, the seedling was learning to simply be.

The Process

There is beauty to be found in the midst of grief. When we take a moment in our pain to allow this beauty to seep in, it can weave a sort of magical thread into our nervous system. It starts as we begin to accept that breaking open offers opportunities for growth. Feeling and being witnessed waters and warms us into life. As the seed planted deep into the dark soil aches as it cracks open, and is nurtured by the nutrients in the soil, receives refreshment and expands as it absorbs the rain, and grows toward the warmth of the sun above; we too, can grow toward the light and warmth of the sun found in the kindness of empathetic others who witness us. We begin to see the darkness of the soil we were planted in may, in fact, provide the environment for us to crack open and begin to grow again. The cracking open can be painful and scary, but it is necessary if we are to heal and grow. While I agree with those who say we are not broken and in need of fixing, I would counter with a different concept of being broken. The breaking away from our old outdated protective shell may be just what we need to grow – a breaking versus being broken, they are different.

As so many grief specialists point out, we cannot heal if we do not feel. We will, on the healing journey, feel the pain of opening. We will shed our outer shell and be nourished by it as we grow. As we are refreshed by the waters of wisdom, self-compassion, and grace, we find strength to move toward the warm sun. As we grow stronger in the warmth of empathetic witnessing, we too, become a thing of beauty that others can look upon for support and nourishment.

They will not see the seed we grew from, the cracking apart of our former self. They will not see what lies beneath the soil as our roots spring forth and grow deeper into the dark soil, holding us upright. They may not witness the fact that deep inside the soil, there is a different type of growth. One where our wounding exists and has created a different sort of evolution. It reaches into dark places to hold us up as we grow into the young seedling witnessed on the surface. They do not see the battle to move through hard soil, around rocks, and the strength we are forming as we grow roots, holding on deep in the dark soil so our outer showing can stand tall.

It is here in the dark soil where the environments we grew up in show their face. Grief tends to bring up unhealed wounds from our past. These show up as reactions, as our protective parts experience perceived similarities in our current environment. These parts may once again experience judgment, anxiety, addiction, dissociation, disconnect, perfectionism and whatever else came to keep our younger self safe. As we sit with these in the dark places, learning to acknowledge them and nurture our hurting inner child, the warmth from outside can begin to feel safe. In this safety, we become more open to hear the wisdom from external sources and grow toward the warmth of their light.

There are nuggets of wisdom we can glean as we open ourselves to the stories of others. The brave travelers who have tread this path before offer a roadmap of sorts, glimmers of hope, and a safe place to feel witnessed. It is my hope that my process can offer glimmers for others as they process their own loss or aid those who walk beside someone who is grieving. My deepest desire is to help others feel seen, and the loneliness of grieving may be covered, if even for a moment, with the balm of being a fellow traveler. You are not alone in this journey.

As we begin to feel the warmth of our supporters, we reach toward the sunshine they provide and grow into a seedling. As a seedling, we shoot upward, seeking more of this comfort. Taking in the world around us, we remember all we have endured, we see others around us who are also reaching to the sun. In our growing we can begin to see the beautiful connection we hold to all others. Loss awakens us to the fragility of life, and it also reveals how each of us depends on others to sustain this growth. Loving kindness from friends and strangers, such as the wind, the rain and the sun, unveil truths of the universe, each of us needs the other to grow and heal. The soil in which we were planted cradles us as we absorb all that we are beginning to witness. We feel our coats burst as we witness the beauty found in connectivity.

Chasing The Sun

The sound of the breeze
The birds and the bugs
Mask the nearby highway
And turn it into a river

The ground speckled
With Sun and Shade
Like an animal
I bathe in its warmth

Resting in the sun
Eyes closed
Hearing the chorus of life
I feel the cool of the shade roll in

I move about
Chased by the shade
I seek the bright warmth
And again, rest

This time observing
The shimmering trees
Leaves falling
Birds moving to and fro

I can see the approaching shade
And chase the sun once more
Working hard to stay within its reach
Before it disappears

October. 4, 2021

The Heron and the Hawk

A bird's eye view
Shows me more of you
Flying above in my mind
Seeking answers I'll never find

As the heron and the hawk
You visit and my heart skips a beat
The longing grows
With fall's song of the passing grackles

I lay awake in the night
Visited by ghostly memories
Intangible
But alive nonetheless

The waterfalls
And wailing
come as they will

And the fog settles in
As the hawk flies low
And somewhere in my heart
I know

Forever mine
Forever ours
Your soul lives above and below

As the heron and the hawk
We settle in the pages of histories divided

Of stories unfinished

In the hearts of our babies
You will forever be alive
In my heart you will dictate the flights ahead

Guiding me with the owls and their songs
The sunsets and the fog
The glorious hawk in flight
You still my fear
If, but for a moment

I cannot see
What is meant to be
What will come of the lives you've left
And I must spread my wings
And rest on the winds

Trusting
Hoping
In my grief,
These wings must hold the weight
Circling
Hovering

Waiting for you to come dance
Dance the flight of sorrow
In mid air
We hover

November 9, 2021

Wind Rider

There is wonder
Everywhere
To behold
We must put down our distractions
And look
Or close our eyes and listen
For the earth itself
Speaks to us
The wind blows
And the hawk replies
With wide wings
With joyous calm
It rides the currents
Wherever it leads
Hovering
Peacefully
With beautiful repose

The clouds too
They shift
Changing shape before us
Drifting slowly
High above the atmosphere
Their shape morphing by the second
And all we need do
Is lift our eyes
To the beauty of the skies
To rest a minute with the hawk
Inhaling

Closing our eyes for just a second
Centering ourselves
Then open again
Sitting in the stillness

November 16, 2021

Be Still, If Just for a Moment

Just under a year ago,
we sat in awe of the migrating geese and their beautiful
conversations.
Winter winds bring the birds from far and wide,
passing over us in a rhythmic dance.
Watching in wonder as they circle back in perfect harmony,
together as one, they move as the breath from my chest –
Undulating,
beautifully awe inspiring.
For a moment, capturing my thoughts with curious wonder,
bringing calm with the beating of their wings.
They move along, searching for warmer weather,
reminding us of the coming cold, the season's end.
Take a moment dear one,
sit in the peace of falling snow,
the migrating birds,
the breezes and wild animals scurrying about.
Close your eyes and breathe it in.
Slowly now,
exhale with the intention of letting go of that which no longer
serves you.
Be still, if just for a moment.

November 24, 2021

Open

I find I see things a bit differently now.
There's an opening within me that looks out at the world
and instead of all the scary I once saw,
I now find myself wading in a sea of interconnectedness.
I think this is something that grief does,
it opens you.
Suddenly, you find yourself facing a world that has changed.
The blinders have been lifted away and you see more.
Your peripheral is now open
and you just see things you missed every day.
There is an awareness of nature that grows –
a broadening of your spiritual scope.
And interpersonal relationships become richer –
you see goodness walking hand in hand with agony.
Where you once saw only ego,
you now notice pain,
fear,
disillusion,
distortion.
You find grace takes on a new meaning
and your method of being gracious expands.
Perhaps it is just me?
Perhaps others do in fact get so lost in their grief they cease to see
altogether?
I walk in that from time to time,
but the birds of the air beckoned me to wake,
to not get lost in the loud accusations of self
and the wagging fingers of blame.
I've read of awakenings

and wonder if that is what this is?
A curiosity about the ways of things.
A less judgmental view about the why's.
Staring humbly down the barrel of time's gun
knowing that this too, shall pass –
like the time with my beloved.
We carry no control over the how or the what,
rather only our response to it –
and that too, can seem to bypass our control,
despite our best efforts.
When you hear platitudes,
dogma,
toxic positivity,
and those railing on others,
you realize the deep human desire to make sense of an otherwise
senseless world.
You close your eyes and feel the longing,
you can literally feel the struggle for more,
for control.
Many would shrink away from this
but there are those of us who have the survivor spirit.
We are a weather worn breed
and we become intuitive as a personality.
We become overwhelmed easily.
We see our scared inner child
and we learn to take hold of their hand.

December 28, 2021

The greatest gift we can offer ourselves as we grieve, is the gift of self-compassion because it guides us toward acceptance – acceptance of the process. As we begin to gain confidence in our ability to move through each day, and we begin to see our actions and reactions as protectors, there is a beautiful shift in our vision. We can go into nature and sit within its nurturing arms. We can learn to be still as our nervous systems begin to trust again in a world that so often has left us feeling alone. The light of the sun stops eluding us and we can close our eyes for a few moments at a time, as we grow our capacity to trust. Our old stories become more transparent, and we can begin to see where we place walls and safety nets to catch us, where in fact perhaps there was never anything to fear. We can also see where there were legitimate dangers our systems intuitively protected us from. The way these unfolding parts of ourselves reveal our inner workings, when embraced with loving-kindness, ushers in a new sight. We can now see, with grief informed eyes, the world very differently.

For Love

Life is filled with tragedies
We must look right into the heart of them
We can't escape them
They are part of the beauty
The opposite side of the same coin
As I relate to those I love
My heart desires growth for all I encounter
As I also desire for myself
No boxes or containers for us
None of us fit
We are too expansive as we grow and learn
Ever changing
To love you
Means I want to encourage you to grow
To expand
This is how I serve you as you serve me
By challenging
Supporting
Sharing
Questioning
Holding
Making space
Sometimes with silence
Sometimes verbose
Regardless of how
It is in love that we connect
"Making you conscious of what you don't see"
Might sound forceful at first
It did to me

like I'm imposing my thoughts on to you
But perhaps if we change our perspective on those words
We can see it differently
Two views come to mind
That of the role of a parent
And the other that says, "You don't know what you don't know"
I always appreciate a well-timed word
Or when someone guides me into a new understanding
Approaches vary
But when done in love
It is beautiful
Life itself does this for us
I am seeing that life itself
God
The Creator
Or whatever life source you believe in
Does this as well
The events in our life are our greatest teachers
Life loves us
We don't always sit comfortably in it
Nor do we always see beauty right away
Sometimes we never will
How can tragedy contain beauty
I believe one is not exclusive of the other
Same coin
Two sides
As an artist
I can relate to the concept
Artists create for various conscious reasons
But I can't help but think there are forces at work behind why we
create

I create for love
To let it out
To connect to my viewers heart in some way
To speak my truths and share my stories
With the hope of igniting your own
Go out in love My friends

December 31, 2021

Surrender

At some point
we are required to let it all go –
if we are the lucky ones, that is…
To look death in the face
as it is mercilessly stealing your love.
No religion,
no God,
no former beliefs fit.
They can't contain what is coming,
they can't suffice.
They do not save as promised.
They do not calm the anxious mind.
They no longer fit
and you must shed these tight shoes.
You must step out of them.

As you free your footing
from what was known,
when you jump from the foundation you once held dear,
there is a surrender that begins to shroud you.
It fills every fiber,
every molecule,
it fills you up as you sit in its shadow.
You no longer feel the need to know.
The questions change shape and expression.
You notice the air,
the currents,
nature,
being,

in ways you could not without the pain of grief.
It requires you to change.

A deep sense of connection follows as you release.
You begin to see that all beings,
all creatures,
all plants,
all life,
rely upon each other.
Even the very air we breathe
fills us with energy
and brings us life.
Energies of those who have passed
remain.
They flow.
They find ways to move along,
to move into,
to move through.
In the surrendered state
we experience them.
They continue to teach us.

They tell you it is bigger,
so much bigger.
They show you how to let go,
to broaden your scope,
to see beyond,
to feel more deeply.
Connecting more fully
they call you to love,
they call you to open.

Open to the things you once feared.
They call you to calm.
They call you inward and outward,
simultaneously.
They awaken your spirit,
sing to your soul,
ignite you.

When you listen,
when you surrender,
they change your frequency.
They pull you toward the whole.
They teach you,
they show you,
they unveil your eyes.
Both inside and out,
surrender dear ones,
surrender if you can
before you lose love.
See it fully now.
Learn from those who learn through pain,
through grief.
Surrender!
Let go!

The only way out, is through.

January 11, 2022

One Coin, Two Sides

Life and death
Joy and suffering
Love and loss
Hope and despair
Together and apart
Calm and unrest
Home and lost
Light and dark
Comfort and grief
Body and ash

Hold on to those you love
Embrace all that is
All that is present
Here and now
Love
Be a home
Be joy
Be hopeful
Be a light
Bring comfort
Be together
Now
While it is in front of you

January 22, 2022

Listen

Listen dear Ones,
the universe is speaking to us.
She has much to say,
if we could stop
just long enough to hear.

Sit quietly,
cradled in her womb.
Listen for her heart.
What does the beat awaken within you?
What stirrings arouse your senses?
What stories unravel
and truths come out on full display?

Does she unveil your humanity?
Do you see the paradoxes?
Are you encountering your capacity to hold light and dark?
To act in both love and apathy?

Does she lift you up
in your darkest moments;
holding you to the light,
letting the warmth of the sun thaw you from the inside out?

Does she show you a world where others can feel your heartbeat,
your goodness,
your grace,
your unfailing desire to live –
while simultaneously holding death close to your chest
where they remind you of your song?

Does she remind you of your song?
Does she pull you to her chest and sing it for you,
resting her hand upon your head as she dances,
clutching you gently,
closely?

Does she breathe life into you,
using the stars to captivate you?
Does she capture your heart,
wrapping it in the salve of the moonlight,
healing you as slowly as you need?
So, you can become strong,
and move from survival,
holding her hand and dancing along with the rotating planets?

Do you hear her call dear ones?
Have you run to her?
Opened your heart to love fully
knowing that grief is the AND to love?

Sit with she and I,
hold our hands,
weep and cry.
Then,
laugh and let her joyous light enter
when you are ready,
only when you are ready.
She is patient.
She has seen so many before.

March 1, 2022

Secrets of the Night Sky

The stars now light the way,
truth now surrounds you,
and the bright moon feeds your soul.
The secrets of the universe now sing their songs
and you understand what this is all about.
Oh, the dark night sky,
lit by constellations,
may it hold space for you,
for us.

March 1, 2022

The Passing of Time

Some days
The sun shines
Illuminating the world around
Casting its beautiful glow
Upon the dormant
Scraggly
Branches
Other times the shadows
Keep them cold
They rest
Taking in the view
Hoping soon
To feel the warmth
To grow
Once again…

March 23, 2022

What If

What if, when your soul passed
it was free to enter any living entity?
What if it rode the wind and found your favorite bird, the hawk,
and entered it –
watching us through sharp eyes.

What if you sat atop light poles
looking down and watching?
What if you were always around us,
always looking out?

What if you were in the wind at times,
and we breathed you in,
felt you kiss our faces,
wrapping around us?

What if you sang to us through the melodies of the birds,
crisp and clear,
soothing our sorrow
even if just for a moment?

What if your energy entered the water of the rivers we visit
flowing through to us and around us,
tickling our toes
and cooling our faces?

What if you could join with our dear Aoife,
kissing our faces with sweet doggie smooches,
or still sleep by my side every night
keeping my cold feet warm?

What if I was brave enough to climb to the top of our land
and you were present in the view,
enveloping me with the beauty that surrounds?
What if you were always here,
even still?

April 11, 2022

The Sky is My Refuge

My eyes are always on the skies
Searching for birds
For the birds bear witness of you
They speak to me
Bring you to Me
They captivate my heart

Hawks and falcons come most
They speak often
Recently, as the birds migrate North
Searching for the lakes and lands they nest in
Turkey vultures are seen

Symbols of death and rebirth
Cleansing
Loyalty and protection

Are you reborn my love
Are you watching over us
Protecting us
Will life be born anew
Our hearts cleansed of shame and sorrow

The sky is my refuge
Hoping to one day meet you again
As a winged creature
Soaring
Flying

April 14, 2022

Rain

The rainbows still come,
the beauty still arrives.
The rain refreshes
and brightens
and makes thirsty things alive again.

June 26, 2022

Messengers

First, the owls came
Warning of what was to come
Harbingers of a story unfolding
That none of us could stop
The two came
Leaving their carnage for us to find
But we were blinded
Not seeing it for all that it was

Then they took you away

And the herons came
Lean and graceful
Medicine for broken hearts
Lifting our heads upward

The hawks weren't far behind
Swirling overhead daily
Landing and watching
Connecting

Then the Grackle flocks
Preparing to migrate
Filled our trees and our yard
Screeching at one another
Loud and in unison
They arrive
And left in one beautiful swirl

The hawks continued
Their territory unchanged
Ritualistic in flight

The turkey vultures arrived
A new pattern drives them our way
Large and mysterious
Protection,
Death and rebirth
Usually together
Save one
Appearing in isolation
Announcing change

Again, the hawks
Always faithful
Always present
Putting on shows
Appearing in small clusters

Oh, the hawks
What messages they bring

August 4, 2022

Breathe Life into Me

The light still shines on my weary, weathered limbs
Kissing the tips of the surrounding blades
The sky cradles me
And life encircles me
Carrying on
Untouched by the loss of you
There is still beauty
But the cold air makes the loneliness that much more unbearable
The horizon nearly lost along with perspective
And the sun that tries to warm me
Blinds me instead
I fade into the distance
A quiet hollowness
Whose beauty still exists
But is lost on itself
Run up the hill to me
I cry
Climb my branches
See me still
Breathe life into me
Plant seeds in me
So I may sustain life once more
Let something of beauty
Take root inside my barren soul
Water it
Nurture it
So it may grow so strong
That it bursts through

Cracking wide open the old, dead shell
Let me live once more

November 16, 2022

Sometimes in orientation, we must find places that feel safe. Often, the old reserves that once cradled and held us as we processed, morph and change as we begin to emerge from the initial shock and pain of grief. We may find ourselves there again and again until we fully process our experience, but each time something shifts a little. Our minds may return to the darkness, yet the light sneaks in and tries to warm and comfort us, cajoling us out. Other times we must find our own warmth and learn to sustain ourselves as we prepare to reach upwards. It is a process and a journey of back and forth, rest and run, be carried and then step out in faith. Rarely is it ever just one thing that sustains us. We must step each step into the environments that present, and bravely dare to keep walking. We must orient ourselves to the light shining down into our dark soil, beckoning us to come forth.

Ethereal Connection

I fix my eyes
on the light just over the horizon.
If, but for a moment
I may draw strength.
That it might look upon my broken heart
and witness the quaking
of memories,
of love lost,
of fears,
and sorrows.
Engulfing them in warmth.
And I draw in a deep breath,
eyes closing as I inhale –
holding it,
holding it still,
and slowly,
ever so slowly,
release.
The sound of my breath,
the wind.
Eyes still closed
I feel the warmth
as the glow of the sun
breaks through my eyelids.
The glow grows brighter.
I slowly open back up
allowing the outside in.
The darkness has fallen to the peripheral
and I gaze longingly at the horizon.

Quietly, I sit in the moment,
embraced by the sun.
I am connected,
but for a while,
to all that is,
and was,
and sit curiously with what will be.

December 5, 2022

Companions

Truly, my lifelines,
I hold on to you.
You, who remind me
I am not alone.
You who understand,
who just know,
who love me
and let me love you.
You who lift me out of my waters when they overwhelm
or let me sit in them without judgment,
holding my head up.
You, who are not afraid of this process.
You, who let my light shine through
even when I fail to see it.
You!
So grateful!
So, so grateful!

January 18, 2023

Unexpected Friendships

Loss can bring new friends.
People who cared about your person
now caring for you.
People who come along and step in,
in ways you'd never expect.
People you want to include in your tribe
because they are simply beautiful humans.
People who make time for you
and allow you to make time for them.
People who make your grief a little more bearable.
Sitting with you.
Hiking with you.
Eating with you.
Concerting with you (that's a word, right?).
Simply just being with you.
I love the unexpected friendships I now have!
So grateful!

January 22, 2023

Supported

Infectious smiles
Shenanigans
Hooliganry
Irreverently reverent
Submit the magic word
AND
Grievances faced
Acknowledged
Felt
Owned and supported

It's all there

The stuff of life

No greater gift than friends who knew the before and after
Who stick around to see what's to come
Those who SEE you all the way through
and hold space with grace and ease

Thankful
Every day
Gratitude and sorrow
Both do coexist

Love you, my friends

January 26, 2023

Tribe

My tribe
I've been collecting you for years
Still gathering in fact
Beautiful humans
Coming in
Going out
Returning
All loved
All with roles still being played out
In this crazy story of life

February 16, 2023

As we journey and grow, we will be able to see those who walked alongside us with more gratitude. The early seasons we needed to be carried and held, and if we were fortunate, we were able to be so. We begin to notice there are those around us who had to carry themselves and experienced very little support. For those like myself, this is heartbreaking to witness, because we know the weight of this load. It becomes so incredibly clear how the different paths we walked before entering this part of our stories has such an incredible impact upon how resilient we become.

The Mallard

Oh, lonely little mallard,
I so relate.
Sitting on a tiny rock island
in some murky water
enjoying the moment when the sun shines on you.

Just so you know,
someone found you beautiful.
It was me!
I snapped this photo
for all to see.

Well, really,
it was just for me,
so, I could look again
and remember you
all cozy in the sun.

A reminder, in truth,
that the waters can calm,
the surface upon which we sit
can reflect back to us
the beauty of ourselves in an equally beautiful world –

Even if the water itself,
below the surface
is murky and dark.

March 7, 2023

Listen, What Do the Trees Tell You?

Trees speak.
If you quiet your mind
you can hear their messages.
They whisper of our connection,
telling us of our nature.
Each tree,
a different storyteller.
Their nature reveals our own,
teaching us how we should live
and reflecting how we do live.

Go!
Sit amongst them!
Explore them!
See how they connect to the earth
and the earth sustains them.
See how they sustain other living organisms.
They depend on the soil, the sun, rain, our breath, and each other.

A perfect reflection.

And we depend on them.

They clean our air,
provide shade,
shelter,
fruit,
warmth,
home,

beauty,
nourishing our very beings.

Listen,
they are community.
They model how to live.

They bend in the wind,
their roots grow strong with resistance.
Those that fall
become part of the cycle of life for other living organisms.
Some grow in their fallen places,
others go back to the earth.
Still, others become homes,
or are burned and provide warmth
and opportunities.

I do not worship the trees,
but I learn from them.
I honor our connection.
I am thankful for their stories.

What do the trees tell you?

May 29, 2023

The Work of Healing

Surrounded
By friends
By the beauty of nature
My little men
With wise words
Stories
Memories

All so patient with this process

It unfolds moment by moment

Doing the work of healing
Reading
Therapy
Reaching out
Crying
Talking
Hiking
Helping

Trying to play
Even laughing

And yet
loneliness follows me
Ever present
The hole he should be filling
The pictures he should be in

The empty bed
The silent end of the line
The spot at the table
The driver seat he would be in
The unreturned emails (I'd text but someone would be the con-
fused recipient)
The missing hand to hold
The quiet
No arms to comfort
No one who just knows without need of explanation
A partner in awkward moments
A place to truly rest
To be
The loneliness follows me

I go silent sometimes (it's rare – I verbally process along this
journey)
My need to normalize this, to allow others to feel seen, is vast
Yet, sometimes, I see the need to stop
To stop needing to be a helper
To just BE where I'm at

Now, is a time to go inward
To process the lonely
To feel it
To be it
To move with it
And maybe through it
I'm not quite sure there's another side to reach

I'm a helper, but I'm asking that part of myself to be still for a
moment

To hold myself
To help myself
To be enough
Just as I am
To make peace with my loneliness
Not looking for it outside myself
But graciously
Compassionately finding a way to give it to myself

Endless journey...

June 20, 2023

Warrior Spirit, Rise

Searching for the warrior that I know resides within.
I cling to nature, friends, and family—
for they are the source of strength.
My love and passion for them drives me forward.
We are all connected in ways that ignite,
creating purpose.
Together, connection to my source is made clear.
I need my inner warrior to arise,
to take up her weapons of love
and kindness,
AND
protection and wisdom.
She is there.
She searches the skies for his energy too,
for he made her powerful.
Though he is gone in physical form,
she can feel spirit calling to spirit –
"Stand up tall! You are strong!"
He whispers.
"Let the warrior come forward,
she is needed."

August 29, 2023

Live

The sunlight danced today,
through branches,
on the tips of the grasses,
casting incredible shadows,
through majestic trees,
lighting the path
for imaginative steps,
and providing joy for furry friends.

These are the moments I live for.

November 5, 2023

These moments of rest, found within the beauty of nature, have been my respite. These are the moments it carries me through the rough patches. Nature tethers me and has become my home. It does not replace Duncan, that place is forever vacant. But nature comes in as a nurturing entity, wrapping me within its arms, carrying me for a spell.

SECTION FIVE

THE SEEDLING: LEARNING TO STAND

Story of a Seed: Part Five

From deep inside its core, the mother plant and all who came before, began to speak to the seedling, "This is what it means to be alive! You are experiencing life! It is a give and take, we all sustain one another. You cannot do this alone and isn't it glorious! All things are connected, we all depend on each other." The seedling breathed in a contented breath and held it for a moment. The intrinsic wisdom swelled, and peace filled the seedling. It breathed out the sweet oxygen and continued learning how to synthesize what came in and convert it to breathe out and sustain the lives around. It was simply too amazing, and the seedling wanted to weep from the realization of its purpose.

"Why did the darkness have to happen? Why did the mother plant have to die?" These thoughts came so quickly the seedling was shocked by their arrival.

"Why are you here? I was enjoying this moment!" The seedling cried out in desperate concern. "I don't want to think about those things!" The seedling felt pain swelling deep inside as those thoughts sat as a stinging reminder of what it took to bring it to this place.

"I can't let you forget! You can't deny this part of your story. It is part of who you are. You are who you are because you were once part of the mother plant." This new voice came from somewhere deep within the core of the seedling. The juxtaposition of the absolute peace and joy at its arrival to the surface and its new-found purpose versus the deeply rooted grief of things lost left the seedling in a confounded state. It suddenly felt frozen and lost while surrounded by all the life-giving energies. It felt like the world was continuing its beautiful routine without the realization of how it came to be. The seedling felt unseen in its stabbing grief. It really did miss the actual presence of the mother plant.

"Oh!" Cried the seedling. "How do I carry this?" The seedling felt itself wilting downward, toward the dark soil. The warmth of the sun suddenly felt a little too warm.

"Psst." A gently nudge from the wind came. "You are not alone. I will bring you some cover." Clouds began to roll in and the emotions of our dear seedling felt witnessed.

The seedling sat under the cloud cover, wilted toward the earth, remembering.

The rains saw the wilting seedling and the wilting seemed to be spreading among the other nearby seedlings, who were also remembering their origin stories. The sadness was growing, and the rain could no longer contain its sorrow for them. It began to cry. Tears fell from the sky and the seedling collapsed to the ground. All the seedlings were being washed in their sorrow and they felt the presence of their friend the rain. They were not alone, and their sorrow was felt by those around.

The soil soaked up the rain, making space for the remembering. The clouds began to roll back, acknowledging the need for the supportive sun. The sun saw the grief filled atmosphere and reached down its tender rays, caressing the seedlings. "You are not alone in this. Remember, growing is not easy. Part of growing is feeling the sadness. It requires that we go into it for a short time, and as we begin to heal and gain strength, we can come out of it. It is a gentle rocking in and out." The sun continued to soothe the seedling and those around. There was a collective sigh, and the seedlings felt the warm hug of the sun.

Deep within the soil, the roots drank in the rain and sent the nourishment up the tiny and growing shoot of the seedling. It began to stand tall under the watchful eye of the sun. As grief began to settle back in, the seedling began to take in the world once again. Slowly, easing its way back into the beauty and warmth; it began to grow a bit taller with the realization that it was surviving the wave of grief. There were new sensations within the seedling, and it was beginning to develop wisdom of its own; wisdom that was growing beyond that imparted from the mother plant. This wisdom came from the discovery of strength, strength to wilt and come back into stature. Wisdom the sun shared and that this experience disclosed to our seedling. It is possible to go into sadness and come back out. Much akin to the ebb and flow the mother taught regarding the weather, grief seemed to carry this same lesson.

The Process Continues: Unknown future

As the seedling, who is sitting firmly planted in the soil, in new realization of the world around and what its relationship is to all aspects, I too am sitting just above the soil taking in the world around me. How do I fit without my love by my side? What is my role now that he is gone? How do I release a future I thought would be and dream up a new one? How do I carry the weight of this loss while opening myself up to future joys and suffering?

It is here in this place that I remember the early days of my grief; when my spirit was open to receive his spirit in whatever form he took. It is here where I remember the way the birds came to me, species after species, catching my attention and calling to me. Birds I had never before seen here in Colorado were migrating overhead. Perhaps I just never looked to the skies quite as much as I did that first year, searching for him to show me a sign he was still watching over us.

Before he died, the owls came. They perched above me for the entire year before he left us. They would sit and watch us. The first time he was hospitalized, I sat in his mother's hot tub trying to work out what was happening and feeling the first pangs of the loss looming overhead. I felt I was not alone and looked up to find two owls sitting in the tree above me. I spoke with them and sensed they were here to warn me. At that time, I did not want to hear the message I felt in my heart. So, I distracted from what my spirit was telling me and took photos of these magnificent creatures. My mind kept wandering to the lore I had read, telling me they were here for my Duncan. As the last months of his life unwound, these owls kept vigilant watch, and when he died, the owls left. I have not seen or heard them since.

I have always been visited by the great blue heron, and he knew of their importance to me. Days after his passing the herons came from high and low, and I felt it was his gift to me. I had never seen so many before. Then, came the hawks, his favorite bird – a bird that would stop him in his tracks. There is a family of hawks living near his mother, where we were living. Daily, they would put on a show, circling above and crying out to one another. We always loved to see them. After he died, they continued, the sightings were more and more common.

One day, while sitting beside the backyard pool watching our boys swim, I was longing for him to be there. A thought occurred to me, what if our lost loved ones could inhabit birds and watch over us? No sooner had the thought crossed my mind, when a hawk came and landed atop the electric pole in the corner of our yard. He sat there watching the boys in the pool for several minutes. I could not help but blurt out to the boys, "Daddy is watching!" and told them of my pondering. We all felt him there.

A few days later, a good friend visited from out of town. I was recounting the story of what happened, when a beautiful female hawk landed atop the same pole and looked down upon us. We both got goosebumps as we felt he was reassuring us that it was in fact him, coming to say hello.

Months later, I had been hospitalized for a newly diagnosed disease. The window in my room gave me a perfect view of the Tower of Memories, a mausoleum located in the center of the cemetery, where Duncan's ashes had been placed in the family columbarium. It was very difficult to be going through a scary diagnosis so soon after he died without him by my side, and this view served as both a reminder that he was gone and was also there with me. When released, it was nearing our birthdays, we were born a day apart. I went for a walk on his birthday and chatted with him about the hawks we had seen weeks prior, asking if they were really him or from him. I asked him to give a sign to verify that I was not just making things up in desperation. "Honey, if that was really you, could you please have a hawk touch me in some way? It can poop on me, land on me, whatever you want, but please let me know." That night nothing happened.

The next day, a mutual friend of ours came to help me with some tasks. During Duncan's celebration of life, we had everyone paint a stone with a word or image in his memory. I wanted to take them to the cemetery. We purchased a clear box and were driving into the cemetery when the largest hawk I had ever seen caught my eye. It was perched atop an electric pole just above our columbarium. I felt him there. As we were placing the rocks inside the clear container, his best friend arrived unplanned. He and the friend I arrived with had once been married, so I left them to catch up for a moment as I went to take photos of this hawk.

A gentleman who worked at the cemetery saw me and told me that many people feel the birds and foxes that frequent the cemetery carry messages. I sat in awe of its beauty and wondered what it was there to tell me. I returned to our friends; my back turned to the hawk as we conversed. I turned to look at it, and it was gone. I noticed people taking photos of something on the ground and returned to the conversation. I felt a sudden urge to duck and felt the swoosh of air pass so close to me as a wing gently grazed my shoulder. The hawk had touched me. Time stood still for a moment as we three watched the hawk fly straight up and away. In unison, they said that was Duncan saying happy birthday to me. I knew they were right. I knew Duncan was answering my question from the previous day in the best way he knew how, with a fabulous display for those he cared about and loved.

The months that followed brought more hawks, eagles, vultures, grackles, magpies, and so many other birds. They all captured my attention in a way they never had before, and I just felt they were all sent from Duncan. These messages were little moments that brought peace and comfort when the darkness of missing him felt too much to bear. These sightings were the sun and the rain seeping into my soil, catching my attention and urging me to continue moving forward, to keep growing.

Inner Child

Climb on my back my wounded child,
I will carry you for a while.
Though, sometimes the weight of you feels a bit too heavy to bear
and I place you on the ground.
While I should embrace you,
I force you to walk alone.
You wander silently,
carrying your own backpack.
I glance back at you from time to time
and I see you struggle with your burden.
Self-compassion calls for me to help you out,
but your bag is messy and heavy
and I don't want to touch it.
I can't.

September 7, 2022

Sometimes we wrestle with what we know, what our environment requires of us, and how resourced we feel to carry our loads. At times, we fail to gravitate toward the light and treat ourselves with kindness because the task feels too big, and we are so weary. The irony is that if we could just offer our inner child kindness, our burden would lessen. Our growth could orient to the light and thrive.

In grief, I had moments where my soul would cry out for me to listen to my inner wisdom, yet I just could not bring myself to act on it. I was weary from the work it took to heal my inner child, the wounds grief seemed hellbent on bringing to the surface were too much at times. I had to set them down and go about my day, all the while knowing they were following me wherever I went. Even in my sleep, I could feel these child parts standing over me, longing to be seen and held. I just could not do it as often as they seemed to need. I ignored those parts often in the early years; however, I began to see they were relentlessly there, showing up in unexpected ways. Embarrassing moments, words misspoken, harsh tones and self-deprecation started to shake me awake to the reality – they were going nowhere, and I had to tend to them if I wanted them to ease up.

I had to listen to my soul if I was to heal. I was not just healing my grief, but my grief was healing me. My grief brought forth the parts of me who always wanted to be seen and held, cared for. My grief said, "Yes, the darkness is difficult, and the resistance unveils parts that need tending. Tend to them so you may feel the fullness of the sun and participate in the beautiful life you have seen. Let your seed coat burst open completely now by loving yourself. This is where I will heal."

You will always miss your person and experience moments of sorrow at their absence. If you do this work, you will also be able to keep walking and growing toward the light. You will learn to live with both sorrow and joy, they can and do live simultaneously. When the sun shines after the rain, lift your head up and close your eyes. Breathe. Breathe and listen. Listen to those around you as they too soak in the sun and as your story enriches them and their story enriches you, bringing you to purpose. We sustain one another. Our sorrow is not ours alone and our story can profoundly impact others. Allow your story to seep out and allow yourself to soak in theirs. Learn and grow from one another, this is how we are meant to live.

Electricity of Living

Surrounded by magic
Hidden by our busy
Carve it out dear souls
Carve out moments
Get out
Get out into the beauty that wraps us
Close your eyes
Inhale it
Open now
Lift your hands up high
Spin as you take it in
Pirouette with the freedom of the moment
Of the now
Listen to the song of the soul within those you love
Sense it now
The connectedness of it all
This begets that, which begets anew
The electricity of the magic
Of living...

December 13, 2022

And Still, I Write

For those who love me
I'm certain at times
my writing breaks your heart.

I know this,
yet, I still share.

I know no other way to be.
Vulnerability is my strength
and weakness.
Sharing openly is my way
and has always been.
But you know that.
I believe with all that is in me
we humans are made to be in connection with others.
Our stories, our truths
are what make us human.

I will not pretend,
painting pretty pictures that don't exist.
When the beauty does show,
you know of its authenticity.
When joy shines through,
you know it's as real as the sun.
My sorrows come as the rains
and my gratitude the light at the rainbows edge.
All the emotions of grief wash over as the tides,
and the infinite sand on the shore a testimony to what churns
beneath.

It's the story of a life lived.

So, if your heart breaks,
it breaks with mine.
If a smile should make its glorious appearance,
we share in the joy that follows.

My life,
your lives,
if they are lived,
will know the balancing power of all things –
beautiful and difficult.

January 16, 2023

It takes time...

This morning, I felt the fear of judgment creep in.
Do others judge me?
Do they think I'm dwelling on this loss and not moving forward?
Do they think I should stop writing about grief?

Then, I stopped.

It's my journey.
It's my process.
It's my lost love.

It's mine.

I've never heard anyone say anything to support those fears.

I'm surrounded by beautiful people who support me in this process.

The fear is unfounded.

I see from my reading that many grievers struggle with this fear,
many also experience this judgment.

It takes time to heal a wound
and the process looks different for everyone.

For me,
I'm learning to walk with my grief.
Some days,

it walks next to me with gentleness.
Others,
it arrives in fierce waves of memories, accusations, and fear.
And some days
I get the full spectrum.

I say to my fear,
"It takes time to heal."
If someone tries to put a time frame,
tries to tell me how it should look,
tries to correct me,
I know it reveals their own discomfort.
I will give myself the grace and space to be exactly where I am at.

It takes time to heal from the loss of a life you envisioned,
from the loss of one's partner and confidante.

If you are a griever,
be gentle with yourself.

If you are a supporter,
gently walk alongside.

January 30, 2023

Public Processing

Why are you so vulnerable?
So public?
No one wants to see a photo of you crying.
Trying to break our hearts?
Seeking sympathy?
WTF?!?

No, none of that, actually.
It's just another part of grief.
If I'm going to help you understand,
if I'm going to help others feel their grief journey is okay,
no matter how it looks,
I need to be honest.

Some days, this is the face of grief.
Yes, past that magical "year" marker
grief still knocks you on your ass.
It just does.

The past two days
I've distracted,
I've avoided,
I've napped,
I've been on Instagram,
I've just felt really off.

This is not an anniversary,
no special time of year,
just an emotional wave.

Am I okay?
Yes.
Am I really missing my best friend?
Yes.
Do I feel like doing this without him?
Hell no!
Do I get up, keep going, love on myself and my kids?
You bet I do!
Is it easy?
Nope.

But really, is life supposed to be easy?
Anderson Cooper, talking about his mom
said she had such a different response to loss;
instead of, "Why me?" She asked, "Why not me?"

I sit with this.

Why not me?
Why not?

In this vast world
every single one of us will experience loss in various forms.
No one is exempt.
Of course, no one wants that reminder.
And yet,
here I am,
speaking it out.

I don't live in that space all the time,

but my grief does seem to follow me everywhere I go.
I figure I better befriend it,
which sometimes means sitting with it,
giving it space to be.
And so, I let it do as it needs.

Some days,
that's creating art.
Others,
watching a show,
napping,
crying,
hanging with friends,
looking at photos,
writing,
cleaning,
immersing myself in study.
Always different.
Always okay.

Brokenhearted AND okay.
Much love to All.
Now, go love on yourself and your people.

February 1, 2023

Labyrinth

You know what grief is like?

It's like that stupid labyrinth game.
I'm the silver marble in the wooden labyrinth
always falling down the damn hole just when I think I have it.
That's how grief days feel –
cruising along...doot-do-do...thump!
Down the damn hole I go.
Never on a steady surface.
Feeling like someone else is in control of the ground I'm on,
never sure which way I'm going to get tilted.

So thankful for good friends who get me out of the dark
underbelly
and place me back on the board.
And for the fact that I have learned to replace myself.

March 28, 2023

Nature's Song

I'm having a love affair with nature
because she asks of me only what I can give.
She allows me to enter as I am
and wraps me in awe and beauty,
creating a space that cradles my brokenness.
She stirs my curiosity and promotes presence in a way nothing
else can.
Providing just enough threat to keep things interesting,
be they beast or storm or fire,
they pale when held next to enormity found in a bird's song,
or the scolding of a squirrel,
or the way the sunlight dances through the trees and lights up the
forest floor
illuminating billions of stories happening just beneath our feet.

She has captivated me,
enraptured my heart.

She embodies the wholeness humanity desires,
the connectivity of organisms is essential for her existence.

And to be part of that
is everything.

She sings the Creator's songs
and nurtures my wonder at the vastness of all things.
She calls to the deepest parts of my soul
and when they surface,
they are not too much for her.

Her energy floods in,
an embrace from her is pure,
free,
unfettered.
She bares no judgment,
allowing what is, to simply be.
Her wisdom cries out,
"You are part of this,
it is that simple.
You are home,
you are mine,
and I am yours.

And when the rocks cry out
you can join their chorus.
For the same energy coursing through me,
courses through you.

Go now,
embrace your neighbor in the same way.
Bring me to them –
for I Am resides in all things,
and illuminates all things.
Many have lost their way,
forgetting that light lives within them,
connect them once again.

Let a stick,
a stone,
a piece of me,
remind you,

remind them,
all are part of something more,
something beautiful and pure.
We are intimately connected."

And so, my affair grows
and expands,
it embraces humanity as a whole.
For we are all nature.
We are all connected.

August 5, 2023

Downtime

I've had COVID the past many days,
which means loads of downtime –
time to think and feel,
time alone.

I wept,
often.

I had no voice
and calls were uncomfortable.
I sat alone in my giant grief waves.

I took stock.
I felt.
I did mental and emotional battle.
At moments
it was very raw –
a hoarse voiced scream into the silence of loneliness.

Recounting the ways grief has changed me,
harboring the desire to recalibrate.
Sitting in shame at the mess that sits inside me now,
swirling inside the vast hole he once occupied –
hardly recognizing this girl.

Praying for a sign from him,
something to say he is still here in some form,
hoping it will strengthen me.

Realizing how his love made me strong
because it made me feel safe.
Partnered with a soul who knew me,
all of me,
and chose me,
supported me,
cherished me,
and allowed me the privilege to do the same.
I was supported enough to let myself simply be.

Now, I have to fight for every step,
every smile,
laugh,
decision,
even sleep,
especially sleep,
is the fiercest battle.
That moment before I let go enough to breathe the heavy sigh of
rest,
that's the most difficult.
It requires that I quiet the outer noise,
the blue light distraction,
and let my thoughts run.
The moment becomes hours
because the processing of grief
is not
letting him go,
but
contending with
what was,
what is,
and what will be.

Because what I envisioned
will never be.

My grief goes beyond losing my best friend,
but also the version of me that only existed because of him.
And while parts of her remain,
new parts arise,
and I don't always love what I see.
So, I have to take stock,
I have to reassess.
I have to let go of what was in a way that allows what will be to happen –
without the haze of bitterness and fear.
I have to find ways to honor what was
by choosing to be brave,
to not give up the parts of me that are
me.

To sit long enough,
quiet enough,
to find her,
to reclaim her.
For she got lost when the floor fell away,
floating in the liminal space,
lost in the darkness between then and now.

That is a scary place.
It's easier to drown out the noise with louder noise.
But, the liminal space no longer serves its purpose
and it is time to find my wings,
to rise into the present space.

September 9, 2023

Chorus of the Heart

As I go further down this path, 27 months feels simultaneously
like forever and "just like yesterday."

My heart is still sighing with longing and painful memories.
Slowly, I'm finding the good memories are returning, but in
chorus with the painful ones. It's a heart song so layered and deep
I can barely believe myself capable of carrying this entire universe
of emotions.

But I do.

I carry them, letting them spill out over the edges of my heart.

To the outsider, it may appear messy.

To me, it's just all my love for you.

I'm not afraid of my love, it is not messy.
I've redefined what messy is.

My fear is that if I stop letting it spill over, others will forget you.
You being forgotten, is not an option.

You were here.
You will always be here as long as I have breath.

I will keep your spirit alive.

September 15, 2023

On Your Birthday

I went for a walk today
To silently talk with no words to say
So, I let the sun do the speaking
Through clouds
And on branches
It came around peeking
And I was in awe
At the sparkle and glow
That every surface
Seemed to be putting on a show
There were moments of peace
In the air filled with the trills of birds
There was no need
To utter a single word

September 20, 2023

Found in the Sun

I get lost sometimes
In the song of the sun
It's gentle notes sweep over the water
The plants
The Trees
The grass
Us
Setting all ablaze in melodies warm and sure
The sun does not doubt itself
It does not question whether it's too bright
It runs its cycle
Day in
Day out
Creating entire operas at every arch of the earth's rotation

September 27, 2023

One Thing Is Missing from These Photos

One thing,
one thing is missing –
the best parts of us,
the parts only you brought out.

You not being here
has dimmed the light in our worlds.
Taking photos of trees you looked at,
branches you touched,
ground you walked upon,
views you stared into – filled with dreams –
dreams that won't be realized without you here to bring them to life.

The memories that flood bring a mixture of warmth and heartache,
thoughts of missed opportunities
chased by one's embraced.

You should be here still,
not memories of sickness, decline, and death.
You.
Your big presence should be here filling up this space,
eating your homemade sandwich in a hammock hung between
two pine trees.
Your axe and bear spray in hand as you call down the mountain,
"I'm going to the top!"
Returning to stand on your log and gaze out over
the tops of the trees,
picturing the view from a window to a home not yet built.

You are missing from these photos,
yet your spirit is with us always
urging us to the land you loved.

Always missing you.
My days start and end with you.
Love you eternally.

October 7, 2023

Sometimes the environment is the actual land upon which we stand. The place they trod, the views they looked across the horizon into, the trees they climbed, the rivers they played in, the streets they drove a hundred times over. Sometimes it is nature herself reminding you that the sun still comes. Even in the storm, it beckons you to rise up with the memories of what once was and sit with what will never be – so that you can embrace what is to come. It is not a moving backward, but a processing and growing all its own. Sometimes we are embraced by the knowledge that in so many ways, they are always with us, and this allows us to carry on with their memory.

I Love You

The first time,
the words came so fast
and with such release!
You said you loved me
and it was funny!

But I knew,
there was truth in the humor of the moment.
You felt you could be the human you were
and that felt safe,
to both of us.
I knew I, too, could let myself be unfiltered.

We laughed together
at the cause of the outburst of emotion,
and relaxed into the reality –
we found someone we could be utterly true with.
It was at that moment
I found my home.

I have been trying to find home within myself since you left –
to make peace with what happened,
to find my inner warrior,
to reparent the scared inner child
and feel safe within my own skin,
to befriend myself.

It's hard to do in the space of traumatic grief.

I took our babies to our spot,
and told them this was where you professed your love.
As we looked out over the city view
the table mountains blurred into lakes,
and the lights into dancing orbs in the darkness of night,
just as they had that night.

Two years and five months into this
and I miss you deeply.
I am finding my inner warrior,
though still pretty beat up
she finds her feet,
every day.

October 21, 2023

Changing of the Season

Healing in the golden hue
I like to take a walk with you
Through the trees we scamper quick
Till a glimmer does the trick
We skip
We run
We have some fun
All while soaking in the sun

Soon the trees will be laid bare
And dormant land will greet is there...

October 17, 2023

Always There

Who me?
Still missing him?
Um, yes!
Yes, I am!
100% of the time!

Every breath I take,
he is there.
When I wake,
there.
When I lay awake at night,
there.
When I sleep and dream,
there.
As I roll out of bed,
there.
In the shower.
there.
Getting dressed and doing my makeup,
there.
Chatting with the boys over breakfast and routines,
there.
Taking them to school,
there.
Coming home to an empty house,
there.
Working, chores, art, teaching,
he is there.
Sports practices and games,

there.
Dinner and night routines,
there.

Always on my mind, in my soul, and beating in my heart,
he is there.
And his absence so much the greater.

October 29, 2023

So often in grief, I get pulled into the past. The memories are what I have of him. It's easy to find myself visiting the old spaces for long periods of time, because I miss him. I miss us. I miss our family unit. I must be careful in those visits because my mind likes to step in and try to resolve the final days, to comprehend what was and what became, and to make sense of something that is unfathomable. It's in these moments I need to find anchors. I need to come home to myself. Coming home means finding my peace – nature provides that.

Anchor

What is your anchor?
What holds you in the storm?
What brings you back to the present moment and out of your
head?

For me, it's nature.
It's the way the sunlight dances
through my window,
catching my eye.
It's light on the branches of a tree,
or glimmering on the water,
illuminating plants,
and casting shadows on a path.

It's the birds of the air,
in motion,
dancing with one another,
resting on a breeze,
skimming the water's surface,
perching on tiny limbs.

It's the wind,
rustling leaves on trees,
whistling through windows,
hair tickling my cheek,
creating waves in the grass,
making trees dance.

It is the energy that flows,
stirring my senses,
awakening me,
whispering secrets to my soul,
connecting me to all living things,
calling me out of my head
and into the present moment.

November 16, 2023

SECTION SIX

PERENNIAL: UNFOLDING JOURNEY

The Continuing Journey

I know this journey is lifelong. I am but a mere seedling peeking out of the soil, looking around at the world, wondering if there will be more signs from Duncan. I am having to learn to lean into the connectivity of all things in a way I simply could not have when he was here with us. Life continues in its cycles and asks me to lean back daily, to go with its flow. It is asking me to trust, despite all that I have seen and bore witness to, despite the fragility of the human mind and body, it is asking me to continue to walk on.

It is difficult at times, as I remember the way his mind crumbled so quickly alongside our dreams. Trusting in life when history tells of death and destruction, also requires that we embrace the great big AND of life. It requires that we be willing to take the risk of stepping into love, knowing that grief and love go hand in hand. Dichotomies exist within nature and we humans are part of nature. We must embrace the facts, life and death are part of the package deal, bringing both beauty and decay. The seed must first transform for a beautiful plant to make its glorious arrival. It literally breaks open as the roots and stem emerge. It simply is the way.

For me, there seems to be various stages in my life that have produced a succession of seeds, seeds which take root and grow in different soils. Each time, these plants carry the DNA and memories passed on from the previous plant, influencing the evolving seed. The seed adapts to the new environments it finds itself within. This seed, the seed of my life with Duncan, has found its way to new ground - ground that feels familiar, yet so incredibly disparate.

Great bravery has sprouted from this seed. It requires bravery to be the warrior who emerges from the ashes, from the hull of the seed. Inside the seed, there is an erroneous sense of safety. It is easy to feel the protection of the seed coat, keeping the outside world out, with its judgments and potential threats. Most of us have learned however, it also keeps out the beauty and love awaiting us. Only when it breaks open and we push through all the pain can we truly live.

So many of us grievers feel a great deal of trepidation about letting go of the holding patterns found within grief. Breaking out of our seed coat can evoke the sense that we are also letting go of our person. It can feel devastating when it feels like the coat keeps them close, wrapping us in the safety of memories. It is the last remaining embrace. Allowing it to break open so we can put down new roots and shoot up to the surface to feel the warm sunlight of life itself, feels unthinkable. It feels like we are abandoning them. And so, we return to the coat, retreating within.

I have seen other grievers race to shed their seed coat, to grow, to escape the pain. Many survivors of stigmatized losses are so used to carrying pain and the act of letting it go feels so freeing. It feels for many like they, for the first time, have experienced their first breath of fresh air and they want more. Coupled with this freedom, guilt seems to accompany many of these beautiful grievers, who are so deserving of the sunlight. Releasing these constraints feels both beautiful and devastating, because this freedom is born on the back of great loss. This duality of joy and grief is so layered and is an underlying commonality for many survivors of stigmatized loss.

The memories of the pain in the seed development, paired with the loss of what formed it, allows us to cling to the pain of the loss. Our loss and trauma are often diminished because others have not experienced the extreme duality. It is not fair to compare losses, for each loss is so entirely different, and for the stigmatized loss survivor, the loneliness that follows the death of our loved one is so isolating. Walking into a world that is so afraid to dive into the topics of suicide and addiction creates a battle of sorts within so many of us.

We understand these losses are outside of the social norm and the nature of them carries the weight of societal judgment. We understand there is an illusion of choice placed upon these actions. We know our person may be judged for how they died. We also carry the weight of belief systems so ingrained in our society telling us they were bad. Even the most well-meaning friends may carry ideologies influencing how they confront our loss. This invisible knowledge we carry places us in a unique situation. Do we disclose all that happened? Do we disclose how they died? Do we open ourselves and our beloved to possible rejection and judgment? The prospect of this can be so terrifying. The lack of compassionate awareness in society is slowly being chipped away as more and more of us tell our stories, and as our collective awareness about how each of us in connection grows. The very act of being human means we will all do things we thought we would never do, we will act in ways that betray our own hearts and desires, we will react to our upbringing and our traumas in unhealthy ways... simply stated, we will make unwise choices. Every. Single. One. Of. Us.

This journey is showing me how the many parts residing in each of us will come out depending upon the stressors and circumstances we encounter, the soil in which we are planted. The concept of choice is so widely touted in many circles, and successful choices are a badge of honor or a goal. While I agree choice exists, I push back a little. For so many people, survival has been such a central experience to the traumas encountered throughout life.

Survival often pushes people into behaviors society deems unfit or of poor taste, poor choice. It is evidence of a culture where compassion and empathy for the experiences of others is lost. The judgments of "They made that choice, it was selfish." Or "You stayed with someone making terrible choices, why?" Or worse yet, we turn on ourselves and become our own judge, before the pain of the world's judgment can break through our seed coat. So many of us sit in these judgments, real or imagined, because that is what we believe is coming our way.

I can say my husband did not choose to take his own life. I am one-hundred percent certain of this. My beloved was sick. He was no longer there. Some darkness, born from survival and pain, took over my beloved. It stole him away. It stole his light. The darkness created a veil through which all he loved was lost. The darkness drove his choices with distorted thinking. It killed him from the inside, out. He died before his body left us. His stay in the hospital and the medications meant to help took him further away. On an extremely difficult morning, the darkness spoke out of my love and said, "Duncan is gone. He died in the hospital." These words will likely echo in my mind until the day I die. He was gone long before his body left us. He no longer had the choice to be with us. I grieved him while his body was still here, I saw him slipping away and I felt powerless.

Carrying these types of fragmented memories can cause us to want to stay tucked away in the hull of our seed. How do you explain to an outsider the events you experienced, and the painful memories tucked away deep in your soul? How do you allow yourself to be brave again and try to re-enter a world that seems so hostile? A world lacking empathy and compassion for the human condition – a reality we know could happen to anyone just like it happened to us? A world that keeps going when ours has been utterly annihilated. What soil can we find to plant ourselves within so that we can bravely peek through our coat and grow toward the sun?

I have found communities of other grievers to be the best soil for grievers of stigmatized loss to find themselves planted within. In these places, loneliness feels cradled and held. Here we can feel seen and understood. Here, we do not have to explain or defend our loved one. It is in this soil where we can begin to soften to those who cannot understand, and we really don't want them to. Understanding only comes when you experience this type of loss, and I would never in a million years wish this upon anyone.

As I find myself in this new soil, and my roots continue to push their way through the darkness beneath the surface, the tiny seedling I have become continues to move toward the light. I bend with the wind, wilt in the heat of the overbearing world, drink in the rejuvenating waters of kindness and grace, seek the suns wisdom to grow me taller, and learn to trust the other plants and animals surrounding me to do their own growing, so we can all learn to live compassionately.

My journey outside the safety of my seed's coat and into the world as a brand-new seedling is just beginning. I know many more epiphanies, lessons, beautiful and painful moments, and difficult growing spells will come. I know the mother plant will continue to speak her wisdom to me, while I gain insights of my own found in the world above the soil. I know the connectivity of all things will continue to unfold as I continue to trust.

My greatest wish for you, my fellow travelers, is to find places of hope amid inevitable storms, to allow yourselves rest when the waves of grief are too great, to listen to the truths within, and to treat the protective parts of yourself with compassion so they may grow into the light. I wish for us all acceptance of the ways of life, in its beauty and decay, so we may discover peace is possible in all things. Hold on to the cherished memories of who your person was, remember them with compassion for all their parts, knowing they too did the best they knew how. Our journey is not easy, but that was never promised to us. Go in peaceful awareness that you are seen and held, nurtured by the metaphorical sun, rain, wind, and soil. You are beloved.

DISCLAIMER AND ACKNOWLEDGMENTS:

It is important to note that I do not claim to be an expert. The information shared in this book is a collection of knowledge gained through vast amounts of reading, courses taken on the nervous system, a year of classes leading to a counseling degree, and personal experiences. I swim in an ocean of experiential learning, and I am forever a student.

I am influenced by Bessel van der Kolk, Gabor Mate, Peter Levine, Richard C. Schwartz, Sara Baldwin, David Kessler, Megan Devine, and Tara Brach, whose teaching and writing I have consumed. They are my chosen teachers, and I am forever grateful for the knowledge they disseminate. I also must credit my own therapist, Valerie Lorig, for her guidance through my many ups and downs and guiding me back to myself.

From Bessel van der Kolk, I have sat in the wisdom of his incredible best-selling book, *The Body Keeps the Score*. His insightful teachings on the ways trauma impacts our brains and bodies have allowed me to curiously explore my own survival behaviors and my struggle to feel safe within my body. He has also helped me begin to grasp how my traumas impact not just my emotional reactions and hypervigilance, but how this impacts my hormones and immune system.

Gabor Mate was another discovery, first suggested to me by my therapist, his work mirrors and builds upon van der Kolk's work. His discussions on podcasts and found on Instagram have guided me along in this journey of self-discovery.

The work of Richard C. Schwartz introduced me to *Internal Family Systems*, wherein I learned about our many *parts* and how they come to protect us. This influence is reflected in *Section One, The Process*, in the line, "...we sit with our internal family – the many *parts* of our self..." and several lines that follow. I do not use Schwartz's specific labels for these parts, as I have personalized and named the parts as I have experienced them. You, my reader, will have your own specific *parts* reveal themselves.

Peter Levine has been on the cutting edge of Somatic Experiencing, helping individuals process their trauma. His gentle and compassionate approach have felt like a warm blanket on a rainy day. His book, *Waking the Tiger,* was my companion on many walks during graduate school as I sought a degree in addiction counseling. I was so grateful for Audible books, so I could hear the book while moving my body, a staple on my healing journey. Levine's work helped me to see how my thoughts and actions were related to traumatic events and offered exercises to help me as I encounter stimuli that overwhelms me. Realizing our very human impulses to act for our own survival come from places written deep within our DNA. His work is both freeing and full of compassion.

Sara Baldwin has been an incredible Instagram find, and her work with our nervous systems has often been a breath of fresh air as I struggle to understand why I do the things I do and why I cannot seem to change the things I notice. I took her course, *Navigating Your Nervous System,* and found so much freedom as I deepened my understanding of fight, flight, freeze and fawn. Discovering I have lived most of my life in a freeze state of survival has been incredibly eye opening and has given me a much larger capacity for grace and self-compassion. I quoted Baldwin in the poems, *Just Be* and *Nature's Song*, in the line "We too are nature." This came from her Instagram, @Sarahbcoaching.

David Kessler was among the first grief experts I discovered after Duncan died. My therapist intuitively directed me to his work since his own son died by suicide. The love he has for all people authentically pours out of him as he offers guidance to grievers and those who have grievers in their lives. His work with Elisabeth Kubler-Ross helps clear up the widely misunderstood "Stages of Grief." It was reading his work where I realized the stages were in fact written from observations of patients facing the end of their lives due to cancer. It was not intended to be a checklist for individuals experiencing grief from the loss of a loved one. Kessler's work unveils the truth of the process of grief, it is non-linear and ebbs and flows differently for each griever with no set timeline.

Megan Devine was the second grief expert I discovered along my grief journey. I appreciated her frank and honest discussions about what grief truly looks like. I bought her book, *It's OK That You're Not OK,* and its companion workbook, *How to Carry What Can't be Fixed.* Megan's writing and work helped me feel seen as I grieved. I continue to find incredible solace in her Instagram posts and videos. Her discussions on various podcasts about prolonged grief disorder being entered into the DSM-5-TR are part of a very important conversation. My heart soared to hear her argue against making this a diagnostic disorder when it is in fact a human experience. I also worried when I heard this news, because I was afraid individuals would feel they were grieving wrong when their grief extended beyond one year. Capitalism is at the heart of pathologizing grief, and Megan has spoken often about this as she advocates for those who grieve.

Tara Brach is a longtime staple in my life. I discovered her while I was learning about mindfulness and listening to *Insight Timer* guided meditations. I found her approach to be one of the most soothing to my nervous system. Prior to Duncan's death, I took her on-line course, *Becoming a Mindfulness Meditation Teacher*. This course provided incredible insights into the human need for self-compassion. She introduced her acronym RAIN as a guide when facing uncomfortable feelings and emotions. RAIN has been a cornerstone to which I return in moments of anxiety. After Duncan died, I purchased her book, *Trusting the Gold*, and her short and easily digestible chapters helped remind me to trust in my goodness. Her wisdom always helps me find my way to loving myself and others.

In the poem *Public Processing*, found in Section Five, I mention something Anderson Cooper shared about his mom. In his podcast, *All There Is*, Anderson Cooper shares a story about his mother, Gloria Vanderbilt, that has really sat with my spirit and in which I find my mind returning to often. He recounts how she never asked, "Why me? Why did this happen to me?" He said she always said, "Why not me? Why should I be exempt from the pain of living and losing?" These words echo in my heart as I can't help but realize, we are not promised a life of ease, and difficult things are truly a part of life.

In Section Four, I state, "We cannot heal if we do not feel." This quote is used widely in trauma communities. I have heard it from a wide variety of sources, however, it originates with John Bradshaw, who specializes in inner child work.

As I learned about the germination process of a seed, I referenced Encyclopedia Britannica online.

Heslop-Harrison, John. "germination". Encyclopedia Britannica, 15 Nov. 2023, https://www.britannica.com/science/germination. Accessed 5 January 2024.